Your Brain is a Border Collie

Building the life you want, doggie style!

Copyright © 2013 by Dr. Douglas Jernigan.
All rights reserved. No part of this publication may be reproduced or transmitted in any form or by any means, electronic or mechanical, including photocopying, recording, or by any information storage and retrieval system, without permission in writing from the publisher.

Your Brain is a Border Collie
published December 2013

ISBN-13: 978-1494486198
ISBN-10: 1494486199

Cover design © Dr. Douglas Jernigan.
Cover photo by Mark Hood. Cover design by Linda Laforge.

Visit the author's web page at www.BorderCollieBrain.com
Available on Kindle and other devices.
If you're interested in bulk purchases of *"Your Brain is a Border Collie"* please contact through the website.

Printed and bound by
CreateSpace, Charleston SC

Dedication

This book is dedicated to all the pets and their people that have passed through my life for over 40 years. They taught me not to judge, that there is no good or bad, only different and that people who love animals are wonderful.

Contents

Introduction. In The Beginning!... 1
Chapter 1. Defining Moments ... 11
Chapter 2. Our Brains... 17
Chapter 3. Border Collie Brains or One Trial Learners... 23
Chapter 4. The Joss Principle ... 31
Chapter 5. Look At Your Dog, Look In A Mirror ... 37
Chapter 6. Trying To Herd In All The Wrong Places... 45
Chapter 7. Football, Baby ... Bring It! ... 51
Chapter 8. All Fired Up (S.s.b.b.b.b.) Or Dying... 57
Chapter 9. Strengths And Change ... 61
Chapter 10. Bell Training Hannah, Joss and Ourselves... 67
Chapter 11. Doggie D-I-S-C ... 71
Chapter 12. Is This Your Puppy Or Is It You?... 85
Chapter 13. You And The Russians... 91
Chapter 14. Housetraining And Habits ... 97
Chapter 15. Training Them, Training Us... 105
Chapter 16. Goooooals!... 111
Chapter 17. The Rabbit Interlude... 117
Chapter 18. Recycling!... 121
Chapter 19. The Oooooooops Syndrome, or Why We Love Dogs ... 127
Chapter 20. Treats: The Gender Thing... 131
Chapter 21. Love, Baby! Yes, Love!... 135
Chapter 22. Changing The Unchangeable... 141
Chapter 23. Finding Our Own Way...With Joss ... 147
Chapter 24. The Post Person Syndrome ... 153
Chapter 25. A No Fault Life? ... 161
Chapter 26. Feelings, It's All About Feeeeelings! ... 167
Chapter 27. Die ... t. ... 171
Chapter 28. Sex And The Single Dog... 183
Chapter 29. Terrier Bliss ... 189
Summary. Life Happens? ... 193

The fall of 1980 while working cattle at Grand Dad Jernigan's farm. From Left, Dr. L. D. 'Dad' Jernigan, Dr. Doug Jernigan, Loyce 'Granddad' Jernigan, Dr. Tom Jernigan with Brown Dog. Dad and Tom got to work the 'front end' of the chute. Being a small animal practitioner, I got to work the "back!"

Photo by Ginny Weathers©

Introduction
In The Beginning!

I'm a veterinarian, the eldest son of a veterinarian. I grew up with animals. Born in 1946 in Minnesota, I grew up in the Flint Hills of eastern Kansas. Yes, just so you know, the eastern one-third of Kansas has trees, lakes, rivers, streams and hills. The western two-thirds of Kansas (from where Dorothy and Toto surely left for OZ) is where the buffalo roamed and is truly, "grain bin windy, big sky country"! I attended the schools in Council Grove and Kansas State University, receiving my DVM in 1970.

My summers during those years, both high school and university, were spent on farms in the hay fields learning the typical Kansas work ethic, "if you are going to work, work hard but work smart." We also all learned the mottos, "if you are going to do it, do it right. Measure twice because you can only cut once. Look before you leap!" among others. My training was traditional.

The 1950's and 60's in Kansas were good to my friends and me until Viet Nam happened. I served two years as a base veterinarian (USAF) in Dover, Delaware. Some of my friends came home in a box. Because of my service, I was able to use my G.I. bill to guarantee an SBA loan and purchase a small animal practice in Topeka, Kansas. Since then, I have spent my life as a veterinarian working with pets and you, their people.

Primarily, I'm writing to let you know that your life can be anything you want it to be. I know this is trite, but your dogs and cats have taught me a lot about you and me. What I have learned from them has dramatically improved my life and its relationships. What they have taught me has helped define who I am today and how I view my future. By the end of this book, you will have been exposed to what I have learned through these experiences with you and your pets over 40 years. You'll get to see what I have seen and learned from my side of the exam table.

First, I feel that your pets want you to know that you, you and only you, are the entire focus of their life. You are not just unique to them, you are special. Your pets would also tell you that if you want something, you must take action and do it now. They know that mice, rabbits and squirrels wait for no one.

While we can't possibly be everything to each other, we are everything to our pets. They want us to have the life we want so they can share it with us. They love it when we are happy. Their joy is to keep us happy, to keep their relationship with us secure, to keep our lap warm, warn us of potential harm, make us laugh and play with us. They provide us with a companionship that no human can. Only our pets can show us what unadulterated hero worship and unconditional acceptance really is.

Secondly, this will be a short legacy to my clients, their pets, my siblings, children, grandchildren and great grandchildren. It contains many of my attitudes that have been developed over nearly 40 years, beginning with the college of veterinary medicine and these short decades of practice. These attitudes were shaped by a lot of resources, but they have been refined by you and your pets. It seems that we never have time to talk about life to those that are important to us, so this is my way of documenting some of the highlights. I hope you'll find this as interesting to read as it was for me to live through it.

A few years ago, I had a client in the office that was in her late 20's. She said to me, "Dr. J, I first met you when I was eight years old and my parents brought me in with my first pet. My daughter is now eight years old. We have just selected her first pet and have brought them in to meet you for your care and advice."

This was a great moment for me, personally and it really made me smile. I had worked with generations of humans and pets. It validated what I had been taught: that if you work hard and provide good quality medicine with excellent service, you can succeed. This client told me in a direct way that at some level I have succeeded. The technology has changed since this young mother had her first pet in my office. The relationships we have with our pets, the human-animal bond, have not changed. In fact, in today's high tech, low touch world, our pets have become even more important to our emotional and physical health.

I enjoyed meeting her daughter and their new four legged family member. On the other hand, her daughter represented the beginning of a third generation of humans and pets. The point was made and it was the easiest, most pleasant way I have ever been told that my hair is turning gray for a reason. In that instant, I realized that it was time to write this book.

Part of that *graying hair* incident was the realization that some things in my life were changing. After I had been in practice for about 2 years, I had a very bad day. It was a new puppy in front of me being all wiggly tailed and floppy eared. Suddenly, out of nowhere, it dawned on me if I was successful in practice and lasted awhile, I would probably be the one that eventually had to euthanize all the wonderful puppies and kittens I was meeting and caring for. For a young veterinarian, this realization is the definition of a bad day. The enthusiasm and joy I had experienced with your pets faded in an instant. It was one of those 'thunderstorm over the sun' days that the Flint Hills are known for. However, in spite of that realization, there were pets to care for and I adjusted. I learned to focus on the joy of the new relationships and let the potential pain of the future wait until it occurred. Learning to live in the 'now' is important. Focusing on the joy and dealing with the future when it arrives is important. Our pets can teach us how important this is! These are wonderful creatures and my enthusiasm returned to normal. However, when my wife and I moved to Canada, her home country, after nearly 40 years in practice, the primary reason I didn't relicense as a practicing veterinarian was that I had euthanized enough of my best friends.

I always loved your pets. I just knew there would be a bad day in the future for all of us. What made these 'end of life' events bearable for me, I call the *dilution effect*. We'll deal with euthanasia later, but when *that* time came for your pets, you and all the other owners had to go back home with only memories meeting you at the door. Your daily routines had been ripped apart. Joy had left. Nothing would ever be the same. I, on the other hand, after we tearfully hugged goodbye, went on to a patient needing help or a new puppy in a child's arms. These events helped to *dilute* the immediacy of my own stress over saying good-bye to one of my four legged friends and the change in our relationship.

In spite of the training I have had, I have never felt adequate helping you in your grief. The memories of my grief with the death of my own pets is always lurking in a remote corner of my brain ready to spring forward with all of its remembered pain and tears. All of your veterinarians and their teams are similar. They love your pets and, at some level, they love you. Clients that reminded me how much they cared for me and my teams made it a bonus day. Can you say cookies at Christmas?

Euthanasia or excellent palliative care is truly the last loving thing we can do for our pets when it is time. We have fed, protected, enjoyed and loved them to a very unnatural old age. We are responsible for all the love they have given us and we have to be responsible enough, in love, to make sure they don't suffer at the end. We can never replace our pets we have lost or avoid the pain, but we can fill the hole in our hearts with another when it's time. An experience I had a few years ago made me question if we have even truly 'lost' them.

I have had several clients relate to me that after a pet had died, they came back to them in a dream or a vision. These pets always had comforting messages for their owners. They weren't in pain anymore. They could see again. They could run, bark, chase rabbits or make mice scurry. The messages had similarities in that even though death had separated us from them, everything was okay. Most importantly, they would be waiting to greet us when we die, as they did waiting for us when we came home from work or school.

The story I am about to tell you is very personal. Some of you are now thinking, "Oh, come on, please, give me a break!" Others of you may think, "I hope this is true." However, I suspect few people have had the experience that I did and in nearly four decades, it remains the only one I have ever had. At the urging of some close friends, I decided to share this story. You can draw your own conclusions.

Several years ago, my clients brought in their little black fuzzy terrier type of dog. I had cared for him since he was a puppy and now, he was very old. He was blind with cataracts, deaf and too weak to walk. Lifting his head was an effort. He could barely wag his tail but it did thump a few times when he knew I was there. He wasn't in any pain. He was just worn out, finished. It was time to let him go.

I gave him a sedative so that his last memories were the warmth and security of his owner's arms as they sat in my office. They continued to hold him as he went to sleep and began to breathe evenly. They accompanied me to give him the second intravenous injection that would end his life. This fluffy little piece of the canine world was sleeping soundly as I gave him the second injection. He took a deep last breath and was gone.

Instantly, as if looking through a window, I saw this same worn out little body at the edge of a meadow jump up, shake hard, look around and start running through the wildflowers. He looked so happy, healthy and free! First, his head was up sniffing the air and then down on the ground trailing something in true terrier style. He was roaring through the meadow and then, the vision was gone. I was emotionally stunned. The contrast was so great from that worn out last breath to the exuberance of what I had just seen that it made me cry. When I shared what I had seen with the owners, we all cried. Our pets leave such a hole in our lives.

What happened here? What does this mean? Was it real? Why this little dog? Why at that time? Why me? Why these owners? There are no logical or rational answers to these questions. Our pets we have lost continue to live in our memories, but maybe they are just waiting to greet us when we die. Our pets make our lives better.

Fortunately with today's preventative medicine, excellent diets, parasite control and not letting them run loose (being responsible pet owners) they should live well toward 15-20 years old, barring unusual medical events and depending on the size and breed. When clients bring a new pet to our office, I used to ask them, "Your new pet should live 15-20 years. How old will you be in 15-20 years?" The point being that it would put into perspective the responsibility ahead and the time involved. Eventually, a younger client asked me, "More to the point, Doc, how old will you be in 15-20 years?" Oh, oh, now it was personal. If the two new kittens we acquired about that time, Tucker and Pippin, lived until they are 18, like our Todger did. I'll be 77 and that's in human years. Hopefully, they'll live longer than that.

"Your Brain is a Border Collie," evolved from living with a Border Collie named Joss. She wouldn't have been a working dog. She had all the energy and instincts but on the fifth throw of a Frisbee, she would consistently have a motor seizure. So, as a working dog, she had no future. We were lucky my wife picked her out of a litter and so was she. A quick note: Border Collies are not pets. They are farm machinery. Like farm machinery, they have unique maintenance requirements and require special conditions to be happy. Think twice before getting a Border Collie or a Jack Russell Terrier as a pet. They love to work and play. They don't do couch potato well.

All of your pets will show up in this book. You'll recognize them. Their eyes, their tails or lack of one, and what they did with you on a daily basis will come right back into your mind. Why? Because your brain is a Border Collie. Your brain hasn't forgotten them and is ready to bring corral them all in a second. These relationships, past and present, are embedded in the neurons of your brain. This book celebrates what is right about us, our pets, our relationships and what these four-legged beings can teach us two-legged ones.

My Dad, as I said, was a practicing veterinarian. Council Grove, Kansas, the community around us always called him, Doc. I was the eldest son and was soon called, Little Doc. So it shouldn't have been unusual to find me drifting into becoming a veterinarian. Like the community, I had a lot of respect for my Dad. As his father loved what he did, my father loved what he did. This chapter's photo is of 3 veterinarians and a farmer. Dad's Dad was a farmer. He was really a dirt farmer. He loved working the soil, planting the plants, watching everything grow and change. He loved battling the insects and, unfortunately for my Dad as a youth and us later, he loved for all of us to walk through his cornfields hoeing weeds by hand, and actually with a hoe, when the corn was too high to use machinery on. What Granddad instilled in Dad became a part of my siblings and me. We all learned to love what we did for careers.

I have seldom seen my Grandfather more excited than the day when a thunderstorm was fast approaching from the west. He took us outside on the east porch of the house to watch the cornfield across the road. What we saw was amazing! As the storm approached the wind and humidity was coming up and the temperature was going down. The broadly pointed leaves on the corn stalks went from being nicely curved and pointing toward the ground to going straight up and creating a funnel that could receive the rain and run it down into the plant for storage. In a matter of minutes, a fifteen-acre cornfield went from looking like a cornfield to looking like a Pentecostal worship service. My Granddad was happy. He loved what he did.

Dad and his Dad didn't always agree on issues or solutions. But they both had the same trait: they loved what they did! I don't know if that trait is genetic or taught, but it helped me make choices about my future when I was young and, now, for what is ahead.

One of these choices came for me during a defining moment when I was in high school. I was watching "Doc" pull a calf in the middle of a January night. Read that as 'Canadian arctic cold'. We were in a pasture in the beam of the headlights in a wind-driven snowstorm. I watched him have a truly great time. The steam was wafting off his head (he hated hats), sweat running down his nose, concentrating on what he was palpating, as he was up to his shoulder in heifer. He was in his element, living in the moment and having fun.

I, on the other hand, was sitting in the passenger seat of the cab of his truck, warm and safe! I distinctly remember thinking: "This is nuts. What am I doing out here in the middle of the night in a blizzard? How can he be enjoying himself?" I can recall that image and feel those feelings anytime I want. It was a career defining moment. No snowstorm January nights for me. No 'up to my shoulder in heifer' for me. Defining moments have an impact! Every decision we make changes our future.

Dad, on the other hand had a client's healthy heifer and a nursing calf. Like his father before him, he was doing what he loved. My brain has never forgotten that event. Obviously, I didn't become a large animal practitioner but I can still see my Dad having a good time in the snow. The pasture this occurred in is now part of the *Tall Grass Prairie National Preserve*. It's the same area of the Flint Hills south of my home town in which William Least Heat-Moon based his book *PrairyErth*.

My younger veterinarian brother Tom, however, has the same passions as Dad. He loves being outdoors in the rain, snow, ice, mud, dust, wind and bugs. A great day for Tom is a day outdoors with country people and their animals. He couldn't wait to go back to Council Grove and follow in Dad's footsteps. Tom isn't a clone of our Father but, today, he's the "Doc" in the Flint Hills and loves what he does. Thankfully, because of Tom's choices, I never felt very guilty about not going back home to follow in my Father's footsteps.

When I finally got into practice, I found that I enjoyed the animals, but all of you really weren't on my radar. In general, veterinarians practice their learned skills on animals but look to you, their owners, for their emotional and financial validation. The patient's health comes first. Your satisfaction is second. In many respects, pediatricians and small animal veterinarians have the same style of practice. Our patients can't tell us much, so the histories come from the 'parents.' Even today, veterinarians and their teams are attracted to our career field because of animals and generally aren't taught much about you. I have spent the last 30+ years learning about you, the two-legged animal on the other end of the leash. I have learned that human beings are very unique. Human beings are an impact species. Pets don't judge us. They just love their human beings, even those of us that don't deserve their love.

While I didn't really care much about you decades ago, your pets taught me that there is something worthwhile about you and me. We have redeeming qualities even if we don't believe we do. Our pets see the good things in us (besides treats!). We need to know these things about ourselves. We need to know what it is in us they see that enables them to love us so unconditionally. Or perhaps, we just need to learn how to love unconditionally, as they do naturally.

I have also learned that, "I teach best, what I most need to learn." (*Illusions*, J. Bach) So, I just had to tell someone what I'm learning. In the telling, I'm learning even more. I do know that if you act on what you find here, your relationships with your pet and the rest of the world will never be the same!

The choice to act on this information is yours. If you act, these relationships will improve. This is what we are going to explore.

Each chapter has some *Dr. J'isms* listed after it. They are condensations of attitudes or related attitudes that were expressed in that chapter. They may not be accurate, however! After the *Dr. J'isms* you will find a *Fun Page*. If workbooks appeal to you, each fun page delineates some actions you can take to apply the principles found in that chapter. Really, these are fun pages that can help you train *your Border Collie brain*! So, get a journal that you would like to write in and get ready ... to go!

Dr. J'isms

1. We all had a life until this moment.

2. Every decision we make changes our future.

3. Life is happening.

4. Is life happening to us or are we making life happen?

5. The only control we have in life is how we respond to what happens.

6. Bad days happen. Focus on the good and the bad will fade.....in time.

7. Are doing what we like and liking what we do, the same thing?

8. Animals make great companions, people take some practice.

Our pets like us, shouldn't we like ourselves?

INTRO FUN PAGE
In Your Beginning!

1. Spend 20 minutes thinking about how your past has formed you today and write down 3 events that had an impact on your life with the understanding that there is no good or bad ... just different!

2. Your past actions created your life today. Today's actions will create your life for tomorrow! On those 3 events, ponder what you did, why you did it and the outcome. Learn from it!

3. List the names of the animals that are or have been in your life and just remember. Remember the joy, the fun and the acceptance they brought into your life. Then, start smiling at the humans in your life just like that and you will be amazed at how your feelings for people will change. As you begin to 'love' people as you did your pet, you will begin to truly 'love' yourself and the future you want will happen!

"Lions, Tigers and Bears, Oh, My!"
From top to bottom: Mardi Growler, Lion; Princess, Tiger; Ozzie, Russian Grizzly Bear. A few of the residents of the former *Lightning Ranch and Wildlife Preserve*. This USDA certified exotic rescue was the passion of my daughter Staci and her husband, Lance.

Chapter 1
Defining Moments

Tigers in school created another defining moment for me. It occurred when I spoke with a group of Infectious Disease Control Directors about you and your pets visiting their hospitals, nursing homes, and schools. These individuals have authority. If they say, "Not in my facility", It doesn't happen! During our discussion about infectious diseases from your pets, a very different topic came up. In their community of 300,000, there was no city ordinance to control exotic pets for 'show and tell' in the school classrooms. Yes, we were talking about lions, tigers and bears, oh, my!

An educational group, with the best of intentions, was bringing young tigers into the schools and doing lessons with the children about these beautiful creatures. The discussion that followed helped me realize for the first time that humans WERE different from dogs and cats, even the BIG cats. It really was the event that began the process that is ending in this book.

As background, you have to know that veterinarians usually come down pretty hard on the side of genetics as a determiner of behavior, not the environment. It's the old, "He's a chip off the old block!" type of attitude. Nature takes precedence over nurture. We know that, unless trained out of it, English Pointers, point; Labrador Retrievers, retrieve; Beagles and Basset hounds are a nose on four feet, Dachshunds are bullheadedness on a leash, Chihuahuas are teeth with a tail and cats are, well, cats, whatever their size, and yes, Border Collies herd!

We have all heard of well meaning, loving couples that adopt children. Some of them have turned out totally different than expected after having grown up in a great nurturing environment. This usually results in heartaches, property damage, and even prison sentences. We have, also, read stories about children growing up in the midst of hellish environments. These were environments that were mean. These children were deprived of love and basic care. They were abused and neglected, yet, they turned out to be absolutely wonderful human beings with great accomplishments. What is going on here?

Your behavior will usually be attributed to how you were brought up. However, in the identical twin studies, where the twins were separated at birth, show that behavior and choices are remarkably the same in these twins (not always exactly the same) in very different environments. So, until this discussion with these infectious disease control directors, I believed that human behavior, to a remarkable extent, was determined by genetically hard-wired tendencies, just like your pets or any other mammal.

So, sitting at a circled table in a conference room, these meeting participants felt these tigers were a risk to the kids. Some of us would be more concerned about the kids being a risk to these endangered species. However, I knew that these tigers wouldn't know what a wild environment was and had been hand raised with a family and their children in their home for several generations. After listening to the discussion for a few minutes, I realized that there was an issue we didn't agree on. In context, I want you to understand that these are opinionated people, are well educated and used to having their way in their facilities! The discussion was intense, but congenial. I asked them, "Which is more important in determining behavior, genetic tendencies or the environment?"

The answer was quickly unanimous. They all agreed that environment, or nurture, was the critical factor in determining behavior. Now, I felt that, you know, pointers, point, retrievers, retrieve and Border Collies herd however they are raised. The group felt that environment, or nurture determined behavior and I felt that genetics, or nature, determined behavior. When confronted with the facts about the upbringing and training of these young tigers in that family environment, they quickly threw out nurture and cited genetics as the determining factor. "These are wild animals, young children look like food, you can't tell when tigers might 'snap' and kill or maim something."

When I asked them why they flip-flopped on the issue, they said that we (humans) could control our behavior, animals could not!

It is true that untrained animals are uncontrollable. And, it is true that sudden 'surprising' motion might activate genetic behavior in big cats. Ask Siegfried and Roy! House cats that are pets will also react the same way. The scars on my or any veterinarian's arms are testament to that! So, if you wondered, we all agreed that having lions, tigers and bears walking up and down the aisle of school classrooms wasn't a good idea. New 'win-win' regulations were going to be written in their community that would allow education, but no risk to the children from the big cats, or to the big cats from the children!

On the two hour drive home, I began pondering the discussion and (as defining moments will motivate you to do) realized that contained within our heads were both the *trainers*, the executive centers or high road of the brain, and the *big cats*, the reptilian brain! What a thought! We have hard-wired genetic tendencies and the potential to *train our brain* locked in between our ears! Within our brains we have both a Border Collie, our genetic tendencies, and a Shepherd, the Border Collie's trainer. Because of this discussion, I began to redefine 30 years of my beliefs about what I have observed while watching you and your pets in my exam room.

The process I have gone through will give you some insight about your own life and it's potential. While the process was interesting to me, the conclusions are where you will benefit. There is good news for all of us. Your pets have made our lessons crystal clear!

You have heard the line, "Your attitude determines your altitude"? Well, your genetics will determine your behavior, just like lions, tigers and bears, oh, my! Unless you take action to create new behavior. You will live by *default*, not *on purpose*. Your brain at the genetic level, the reptilian brain, is a Border Collie. All it wants to do is what it is wired to do. For the same reason, a Border Collie just wants to herd, herd, herd and herd, from birth until death. Now, herding behaviour is a unique strength, but if there is no training, there is no benefit. If you don't know that your brain is a Border Collie, you will be just another Border Collie and lead a Border Collie life. Leading a Border Collie life is fine. However, when you know your brain is a Border Collie, you can become your own trainer. Then, you can lead the life you want instead of just fulfilling your genetic Border Collie life. Suddenly, you are truly in control of your destiny. The happiest Border Collie is well trained and herding when and where the shepherd wants. It is fulfilling its potential because of the training it has had in its genetic strengths. Does that make sense? If not, it will soon!

In my career I have met, literally, thousands of wonderful dogs, cats and their owners. Our pets have a lot to teach us about how we can go above and beyond all that we currently have in life. We can do it because we want to and with very little stress. Does this mean it'll be easy…no, but it will be simple. Training a dog takes patience and persistence. We can train a dog because we know what action to take, when, where and why. Training ourselves is no different and this book will help you learn how.

However, if you are happy with your life, this book may only confirm to you why you have succeeded. Hopefully, if you decide to take some action on what you and your pets have taught me, you will know how to train that Border Collie part of your brain and lead more than a Border Collie life!

Dr. J'isms

1. Defining moments are only rungs on the ladder of your life.

2. Defining moments have no benefit if we do not learn from them.

3. Good news! We are the most effective trainer of our brains.

4. With untrained Border Collies, herding success is random and unpredictable. Train your Border Collie brain and herding success is assured.

FUN PAGE
Your Defining Moments!

1. List 6 ways that you are like your Dad or Mom or Uncle Dan or Aunt Mary. Then, decide which of these are the way you are or if they are learned behavior. **Clue:** Most genetics are comfortable, easy to do in the beginning. Most learned behavior was hard in the beginning, like learning to drive a car.

2. List 3 *a-ha!* defining moment experiences during your life. Now, write how the passage of time has *redefined* your defining moments.

3. Begin writing an **I want** or an **I intend to have** list on a separate piece of paper and keep it handy. Occasionally read it out loud so your brain can hear it.

    - Write what you want, not what you have.
    - Write all the detail in your 'want list' you can.
    - This will be a long list.
    - This will be a fun list.
    - This will be your list.
    - This will become your life!

Dad's 80th, The Hays House Inn, May 2004
Four generations of genetically connected Jernigan brains.

Chapter 2
Our Brains

Brains of medical people, veterinary or human, rock! When a patient comes to us with an illness, we take a lot of abstract information and distill it down into its essence: a diagnosis. Your brain is no different. It also rocks! All of our brains work this way naturally. It's a survival technique. All of us solve problems. It's a skill that we use our brains for all the time. But most of us feel that we ARE our brains! You know, when you want to do something differently but you wind up saying, "I'm just not built that way! Or, I could never do that and probably never will, etc." We tend to limit ourselves to our brain function and feel like "Brains are us!" At the same time, we don't feel like we are our big toe, our left knee or our kidneys! They are all just a part of us. Our brain is the same.

Our brain is just another body part that has functions that can help us or hinder us. The essence of who we are is greater than any one part. In a morgue, you have the sum of the parts lying on a slab. Who we are is greater than our parts. The brain's parts are many and extremely complex, but only three areas are functional for this discussion. First, the earliest brain part is *reptilian brain*. Secondly, the dog/cat/human *emotional* brain is a higher functioning *mid-brain*. Thirdly, our human, higher 'executive' center, is what makes us different and gives us our potential to change if we use it.

The first or reptilian part of our brain keeps our body running with stimulus in/stimulus out type of reactions. It keeps our temperature normal, our heart working, our liver and kidneys functioning, and our blood pressure normal just to name a few of thousands of tasks this part of our brain takes care of without your consent. Another name is the 'unconscious' brain. It is intricately connected to the next part of our brain.

Secondly, at the emotional level of our brain, we perceive life and react just like our dogs and cats (or horses, cows, sheep and hogs). Our brains are the same in this context. Our brains are no different from Rover, Fido or, quick, pick a cat name, Fluffy? All of our brains are wired and programmed at this level to solve problems for us, to help us survive, and to record pain and pleasure experiences for future use among a myriad of other functions.

For humans, the *emotional* part of our brain is DSL cable fast on response. Dale Carnegie once stated, "When dealing with people, remember you are not dealing with creatures of logic, but with creatures of emotion… " In other words, we *feel* quicker than we think. It's brain science, not rocket science. fMRI studies show that this part of our brain fires more quickly than our executive center. An emotional reaction is normal but learning to respond is the key to success. It is why you have heard it said, "People will forget what you say, but will never forget how you made them feel!"

That is why, when we are startled, our hair stands up on our neck or arms and then we try to figure out why it's happening! We 'freak out' then look around for why. In general, we make our immediate decisions based on emotion and then justify it with logic from our higher centers.

Thirdly, in our higher centers, is where you find logic. This is where we look for the who, what and why. Logic is what makes us human and differentiates us from our pets. It is that increased capacity of our higher centers that allows us to train this Border Collie part of our brains to do what we want rather than living by default!

Many of us, unfortunately, do not use our higher centers to train the emotional, genetic tendency, part of our brains. We live as victims of our internal controls that run in the default mode. They keep us ticking along on a default mode with no one driving the train. We are herding, but most of us haven't found the sheep in our lives. Our herding train track goes straight ahead but there are no or few stations on the map. Have we been living the life we want, or are we living our lives in the default mode? There is nothing wrong with a Border Collie life if that is what you want. However, pets have taught me that as humans, we can do things differently and better in our lives and relationships. These new skills that our pets teach us make a difference!

One of the areas that our brains are similar is that any event that creates emotional responses, good or bad, dumps endorphins into the blood stream. This endorphin flood hits the hard drive of our brain and causes it to pop open like a jack-in-the-box. It automatically becomes a multi-faceted audio video recording machine. This happens without your consent, just like the beating of your heart. Yikes, bang, recorded.

Whoa! That, "yikes, bang, recorded" information, event, song or, you pick it, is buried in your brain forever! Yep, that's right ... at some level – forever. This is why, when you hear a song from 40 years ago that had some emotional connection, if you are over the age of 40, you can recall the first time you heard it. Not only recall it, you will know where you were, whom you were with, what you were eating and how the place smelled. Remember, this happens whether or not it is a positive or negative experience. Dramatic, emotionally traumatic experiences can lead to PTSD (Post-traumatic Stress Disorder). PTSD patients, human or animal, have very freaked out brains. Neuroscientists are doing amazing things today for PTSD. If you know of someone that is struggling with this disorder, find them additional help. It is no longer just about pills. Our brains are amazingly resilient. Our brains really do rock!

Our pet's brains work exactly the same on this emotional or genetic level. This is the level at which our pets primarily exist and function. However, we have a greater potential. We, as I said, are not our brains. We are greater than the sum of our parts. Only one part of us is our brain. However, it IS a Border Collie and it needs training! You can have the life you want, if you want it.

Dr. J'isms

1. Our brains are part of us, but not 'us'!

2. Our brains run on "default", but we get to "choose."

3. We can train our brains, like we can train our pets.

4. We should be in charge, not our brains.

5. Emotions are good. Emotions controlled by logic are best.

FUN PAGE
Your Brain!

1. Reread this section. List the 3 general parts of your brain.

2. List 4 breeds of dogs and what they "do". Example: Border Collies herd

3. List 3 habits you want to change and why.

4. List 2 behaviors for each behavior you must change to kill each habit.

5. List how your day must change to use these new behaviors.

6. List the benefit of changing these habits.

7. Read 3, 4, 5 and 6 out loud daily so you can hear what you wrote and talk to yourself as if you are training a dog as you read.

Joss waiting for the cats, Khali, top and Todger to come down out of the cat haven for herding

Chapter 3
Border Collie Brains or One Trial Learners (Joss, Khami and you!)

The smartest dogs are Border Collies. No one will argue about that. Cats are smarter. Joss, our Border Collie, was a one trial learner. Most of our brains function like Joss'. A bad or good emotional experience is yikes, bang and recorded into our brain wiring. It can lock us into a behavior for life unless we realize we don't have to be just an old drunk or silly as a newt or I never remember anything longer than 30 minutes type of person.

When Joss was a puppy, we took her to a busy park to socialize her to the chaos, noise, children and cars. Joss was doing well, but was a little wary. It was a new experience for her and there was a lot of activity. It was a lot of sensory input for her. There was much to see, hear and learn. In hindsight, for a Border Collie, it was a highly emotionally charged, brain activating motion.

As we walked past a tree, a small child leaped from behind it yelling and trying to grab Joss from behind. Joss reacted as if a cougar was attacking her. Actually, that child was acting like a cougar! There was no snapping or aggressive behavior from Joss but it scared her badly. Her tail was down, her ears were down and she was leaving … now. The park tour for her was over but it was never forgotten. She became an instant four-legged PTSD patient.

After that *one trial* experience, children under a certain age were the enemy. Children were never to be trusted and were aggressively confronted whether they were within close range or blocks away. Whenever we went for a walk and she sighted a child, she would give a low growl and give me a quick look that said, "There is another one of those cougar children!" We spent a lot of time working to help her *undo* what that *one trial* had created between her ears. Finally, we just kept her away from young children, including our grandchildren when below a certain age. That event formed an opinion for Joss that lasted her entire life.

What's the point? Our brains react the same way to any emotional event in our lives. This was dramatically negative for Joss. Don't we have similar dramatic events and do we not react the same way about these events in our lives? How many of us after seeing the original movie Jaws have thought twice before going into the ocean, even the shallow areas. How many of us won't ever go into the ocean the first time? Jaws was just a movie. It wasn't even a **real** experience but if it has an emotional reaction for you, your brain won't forget it.

Take some time and recall one trial learning experiences you have had. Look at the areas of your work, your relationships, your recreation, your hobbies, your habits, your drug addictions. It makes no difference whether they are illegal or legal emotional experiences. It could be marijuana, heroin, nicotine, chocolate, sugar or alcohol. It could be your lack of goal accomplishment, your lack of exercise, your lousy gluttonous diet (I know, you are just too short for your weight!) and any thing else that was, "Yikes, bang, recorded" in your life.

Do these one trial learning experiences from your past control your behavior today? By controlling your behavior, does it control your life? The answer for all of us, at some level and more than we know, is YES! Do these events from our past need to control our future? The answer is NO! By taking action on what we are learning, all of us can create what we want in life rather than accepting what our Border Collie brains are telling us to do! Training our brains is where the present creates the future and the choice is always ours.

An important word to notice while training your brain is this word. BUT! It is highlighted because whenever you see, hear or think that word, the context is changing. What comes before but is different than what comes after and vice versa! It has nothing to do with our pets, but pay attention to that word in your life, it has a huge impact! "It's a nice day **but**" I could have gotten it done, **but**, I should have helped, **but** I could have had his or her success **but** ad nauseam. If you eliminate your buts, your Border Collie brain training will go a lot better! Pay attention to that word in your life.

Our first Abyssinian cat was named Khamsin. His name meant 'a desert wind' and he was. He was very quick and reactive to sounds. Khami was a wonderfully sweet cat. At the time, we lived in an up and down condo with an open staircase. One night he was sitting on our bed upstairs and I wondered how he would react to a strange noise. Some kind of sound he had never heard before. Stupid me! So, in the interest of science (really?) I began to make a soft "wooooooooooooo" sound as I came up the stairs. His response was immediate but cautious. He looked off the bed and down the stairs with a posture that was somewhere in the midst of running, attacking and leaping. He wanted to be a desert wind.

As I came into the bedroom, he looked at me through disbelieving, dilated eyes. It was as if he was saying to me, "Dad, there is a wooooo in this house. I can't believe it!! How did you get by it?" Yes, I was guilty. For days he was cautious near the stairs, always looking around, convinced that the wooooo was near. I have no idea what that sound meant for him, the visual image he associated with it or what kind of terror it held. The wooooooo was not his idea of a good thing. In one small instant of one trial learning, the wooooooo was born for Khami and lived with us until we moved into a different home.

This event helped me realize that most of my own irrational concerns aren't any more real than Khami's woooooo. It's like the adage, "F-e-a-r stands for False Expectations Appearing Real." There may be no rational reason for our feeling, but we just know that the wooooo is close. Any emotionally driven event gets locked into our brains for future reference.

It helps us focus our lives if we will look at our own woooooooo's. When we realize that they don't really exist anymore. When we realize that they aren't valid anymore, we'll have a more joyful existence. When you look into your past or present, you will find wooooooo's that limit us. These wooooooooo's are skewing your decision-making. They are turning your great decisions into mediocre or fear driven choices. They are keeping your life where it is, instead of where you want it to go.

It is worth searching for those things in your life for those things you have forgotten. Those things that have done nothing to you recently and, yet, they control your choices for now and impact your future! It was Bob Dylan who sang, "It may be the devil or it may be the Lord, but you're gonna' have to serve somebody!" Don't spend your life serving your own woooooooo's that have been wired into your brains! Those one time experiences have been recorded on our brains and try to control us. Our brains are doing their job and are just trying to protect us. We have to train our brains that the wooooo's no longer count. We don't want them control our future like they have our past. We are going to find out how your pets taught me to loosen the wooooo's impact, make them disappear and give you control over your own destiny.

Here is another *the dog shows the way* story. Joss was trained not to go up the stairs in our home. Being a dog, she never went up the stairs. If she had been a cat, she never would have gone upstairs as long as we weren't watching! (I love cats but they're not little dogs!) The upstairs area was the cat's safe haven. Joss' brain, being a great Border Collie's brain, was activated by motion. If anything moved, her brain, eyes and ears would light up and would be followed in a nano-second by her body in flight!

If you ever get the chance, you should watch Border Collies, or any herding breed work. The intensity you see on the book cover is the way they exist. Like a light switch, they are on or off. This breed is the poster child for focused action! Jack Russell Terriers are the poster child for ADHD. Be forewarned!

Border Collies are amazing machines with built in motion detectors that activate even in their sleep. Like your motion activated outdoor lights, motion turns on the brain and body of a Border Collie. It is what they live for. Remember, they are ranked as the smartest of dogs.

Cats move. So, Joss loved to herd our cats. Khalifah, our second Abyssinian or the successor, was smarter than the smartest dog. So, for you cat lovers, this is your time to be proud. Joss could recognize Khali's tread coming down the stairs from the cat haven. Joss would then head to the bottom of the stairs (see photo) to begin the game. This game was played at least daily. Now, Joss wasn't a heeler, so she wasn't into nipping. She just loved to get ahead of them and herd those cats. Herding cats, by the way, is futile. That's why the phrase for a futile effort is, "It was like herding cats!" Joss would agree with that statement but since cats move, they get herded.

Anyway, Joss would get her kicks by making Khali change direction over and over again if she could. Todger, a much more dominant personality type, wouldn't be herded. Even if Joss gave him a little go-go shove, Todger wouldn't move. So Khali got all of Joss' attention. To Joss, Todger was very boring.

At the bottom of the stairs, Khali would start to the right as if going into the family room. As Khali feinted right, Joss would dart down the hall to her right, around the corner of the kitchen, through the dining room and flew turn into the family room to 'herd' Khali.

Khali, after starting right, as Joss broke to the left, would turn left, following Joss down the hall and through the kitchen to the cat larder.

Meanwhile back in the family room, Joss would be looking under, around and on top of the furniture She would be looking outside the deck door trying to decide where Khali went. You could see in her eyes that she thought Khali was magical. Her eyes always seemed to say, "How did he do that?" Joss, in her 13 years of life, never figured it out. Khali, the magical cat would disappear every single time.

Joss' behavior, would be labeled a fixed action pattern. A stimulus occurs and a **fixed action** is fired off. For her, this was the never ending game, looping over and over and over.

Now, let's get personal! In many of our behaviors, we are just like Joss. In certain situations our brains have created our own fixed action patterns. Like

Joss, we do the same thing over and over, wiring it ever more solidly into our reptilian brain, and never get the results we expect or want. Do you see where the Border Collie brain between our ears has an impact? Can you see what we are learning? Can you see how we are similar to our pets in our behavior? If I want to change our pets behavior, I must train it. If I want to change my behavior, I must train it. No training, no changing.

If we let our brains just run our lives through fix action patterns, we will have Border Collie, or Dachshund, or Schnauzer, or Rottweiller, or cat lives. There is nothing wrong with that, but we will keep playing the same games with the same results, over and over and over again. How many times have you heard someone say, "Oh, oh, here we go again! Or, I don't understand why this keeps happening. Or, Why have I remarried the same person 3 times?" Like Joss, we have the same loops occurring in our lives and wondered when it was all going to stop, change or give us new results. Well, now, with a little practice and training of our brains, it will stop, change and give us new results. Our cats don't have to be magical!

You already know that doing the same thing over and over and expecting a different result is the definition of futility or insanity. Well, I call it, "The Joss Principle". When we find ourselves repeating behavior that doesn't get the result we want, what should we do?

First, we have to realize that the magical cat did it again! Becoming aware of the behaviors we want to change is critical. Then, we must take action by changing how we *herd* the situation in our lives. If we are herding and there is no cat when we get there, it calls for evaluation. This requires using the executive center of your brain to analyze the situation and create a plan for new action. 13 years was a long time for Joss to be puzzled over the magical cat. How many years do we want to be puzzled over the magical cats in our lives? Do we even want to get it right? Do we even want to get it? The answer lies in training the Border Collie that lives between your ears. Keep on reading!

Dr. J'isms

1. Trauma, good or bad, creates **one trial** learning. It limits us.

2. Because a door was closed, it doesn't mean we can't open it now.

3. Because a wooooooo existed once, it doesn't mean it lives now.

4. To change a **fixed action pattern** you must do something differently.

5. The Joss Principle: Doing the same thing daily and being surprised that nothing has changed.

FUN PAGE
Your Border Collie Brain And One Trial Learning!

1. List 3 or more experiences in your life that **one time** was enough for the rest of your life whether it was good or bad. Consider if it is still valid in your life now and write it down.

2. List 3 things that are constantly on your mind that distract you. Write down how you would eliminate them from your world permanently. Be creative.

3. List 3 things in which you never get the results you want. Next to each, write how you could change the way you will approach them with the next **herding** episode.

Joss

Chapter 4
The Joss Principle

Joss was a teacher. She taught us how to recognize when the Joss principle is occurring in our lives. So, how do we figure out where the magical cat in our lives went? We are approaching brain training central! If you have a real Border Collie in your home, the genetics are immediately evident. You can see them. Actually, if you have a real live anything in your home, including humans, the genetics are visible. Earlier, I indicated that any motion activates a Border Collie's herding instincts. If you want this behavior to be useful, you'll train a Border Collie to respond to commands. You'll teach good working commands such as come bye, away, walk on and good obedience commands, such as, come, heel, sit, stay and lie down. It's the training has impact and creates benefits.

Training principles to apply for humans or pets:
1. **Make the training commands short**, one word commands or short phrases that are expressed with emotion.

2. **The commands must be spoken.** Just sitting around the house with thoughts of: "come, heel, sit and stay" directed to your Border Collie has absolutely no effect. You must speak the commands for training. You must be consistent. You must be persistent. You must be patient, patient, patient and patient.

3. **You must praise the correct responses…** and emotionally ignore the incorrect.Dogs, just like us, respond to whatever gets the most emotional reaction or response because their brains are just like ours…in that genetic/reptilian part.

4. Finally, **you must actually do training…** you must take action toward your goal. Good intentions do not create a well-trained Border Collie or a brain!

We can recognize the Joss principle in our lives when the results in our lives do not turn out the way we want over and over and over. It's as simple as, "Where did the cat go?" It's confusing when we are confronted with the need to change some things. In order to adapt, we must create new behaviors. We must eliminate old behaviors and try to understand why we do things the way we do. Unfortunately, we usually settle for: That's just the way I am. I've always behaved this way. I'll always be this way!

This is called living life by default. There is little hope. It's too hard to change! If you were an untrained Border Collie, a poodle or a smooth faced mix, these comments would be true, but you're NOT! You are a human being and we are different. I can train a dog into new behaviors. The dog trainer for us is between our ears. The dog for us is also between our ears. We can train the dog in our heads.

I love dogs. All veterinarians will tell you there are no ugly dogs, the same way a politician will tell you that there are no ugly babies! But, whether they are large or small, hairy or hairless, tailed or tail less, dogs are dogs and cats are cats! Humans are not dogs or cats, but most of us live as if we are dogs or cats. As if we have no control over our lives, no real choices and no "all fired up" hope for a future we want. Like a Rat Terrier looking for a mole, we just keep digging the holes we have created to a deeper and deeper depth. So let's look at these things.

Dogs and cats fulfill their genetics. Their genetics are always on display. Our genetics are always on display and trust me, I know what I am doing. Lol! When we get to Doggie DISC, you will see graphically how our genetic behaviors are on display to others.

Most of us live by our genetics. We live by our built in tendencies instead of what we choose. Brain function tests, such as PET scans and functional MRI's, show brain activity occurring as our brain functions. Your brain activity increases the most when you are confronted with something new. Anything that stimulates your brain qualifies. It may be a new challenge, a new activity, a new way to work or solving a problem that is different than your routine day.

On a routine day, when you are driving to work like you do every day, over and over, and over, your brain activity is on cruise control or auto-pilot. Your brain isn't a "glow worm of activity, you just glimmer, glimmer! (Read, "Live Before You Die" with its workbook "Oh, To Be A Glow Worm" by Mark Hood). During routine events, your brain doesn't really light up with activity. So, if you substitute the words, MY BRAIN, for Border Collie in our training throughout this book, you will find your life changing! It's logical that if you are going to train a real Border Collie, you must have an idea of what you want the training to do. In training your brain, the same thing applies.

1. **START** by making your training commands one word or a short phrase with emotional connections. If you need action in your life, some good commands would be "Go, Go, Go! I'm all fired up about_____! I want this and I want this now! I'm a Border Collie, a dachshund, a Great Dane, (you pick your breed) and no one can stop me. While training, what I want is my only focus. Either join me or get out of my way! I am an SUV on ice,

baby, I'm going where I'm headed whether you want me to or not!! This is my food, drink and joy! I love what I have arriving in front of me. You're a good boy (or girl). Smart, Smart. Sharp, sharp! Looking good! So, pick your word or phrase and apply it to what you want.

2. THEN you must **speak it out loud** so it goes into your ears, which goes into your brain, then gravity takes it into your heart and then it goes into your feet and hands for ACTION!! Ok, so I'm being a little silly, but can you imagine training a real dog by just thinking about it! No training occurs with your pets just by giving it thought. It must be spoken. Again, on training ourselves, we must be patient, consistent, persistent, day after day after day after day. Human beings are belief driven organisms. What we say, we hear. What we hear over and over again, we will eventually believe and if we believe something we will act on it.

3. AND you must **praise yourself** for what you do correctly. Reward yourself for the good things, just like you would reward a dog while training it. AND, you must emotionally ignore the incorrect responses, the errors, the screw-ups and the lack of action. Whatever gets the most attention in our mind is what we will continue to do.

4. IF we chew ourselves out, say negative things about our behavior with lots of emotion…our brains, our Border Collie brains, just perk up their ears to listen. It goes into our brains, then gravity takes it into our heart and it goes to our feet and hands … for NEGATIVE action and storage. Truly, if you will train your brain as if it were a dog, you can have what you want now and in the future!

5. FINALLY, you have to **do it, do it, do it and do it.** Like all new things, it will feel pretty stupid when you start doing it, but what great results happen! As I said, good intentions, thinking about it, considering it, pondering it, even teaching the theory will not get results. It takes ACTION, ACTION, and more ACTION! Knowing about something is wonderful but acting on that knowledge creates the results.

Dr. J'isms

1. Genetic strengths just are.

2. Trained genetic strengths create success and freedom.

3. We are happiest fulfilling our genetic strengths or, "doing what we are".

4. When we speak out loud, our brain must listen, just like a real Border Collie would listen to his/her master.

5. Review steps one, two, three and four from above over and over and over.

6. Say it! Patient, consistent, persistent! Patient, consistent, persistent!!

FUN PAGE
Your Joss Principles

1. List 3 things you feel you do well. Ex: Listen without interrupting.

2. List 3 things you would like to turn out differently than they usually do. Ex: Being happy when you wake up to go to work.

3. Write down how using the answers in 1 help find the results in 2.

> You don't have to be pretty to be loved

Chapter 5
Look At Your Dog, Look In A Mirror

He loved bulldogs. Pat absolutely loved those snorting, choking, slobbery, sweet natured bulldogs. He once said to me that he loved their personalities and the way they looked. This client had a wonderful personality and great self-esteem. I never saw him appear unhappy or heard him complain about anything in his life. If his bulldogs could talk, I am sure they would sound just like him because his love for this breed wasn't a surprise to me. Every time Pat looked in a mirror, a human bulldog looked back.

For Pat and his first bulldog puppy, it was love at first sight for each of

them. They had instant rapport! In thinking back over the years, I realize that if Pat didn't like himself or have such good self-esteem, he probably wouldn't have liked this breed as much as he did. He did love his bulldogs. He and his bulldogs were classic examples of facial mirror images. Pat liked himself and replicated what he saw in the mirror in his selection of a pet. It may seem odd to you, but our selection of a pet reflects some of our core values and beliefs. Just so you know, for me, it has been Dachshunds. I love their enthusiasm and dogged bullheadedness. When they are on a task, they just will not quit unless physically restrained. It tells you something about me and about my core values. You may stop me or I may fail but I will not quit. If you have ever had a pet and had a hand in choosing it, think about these questions:
1. Why did you have a pet?
2. Why did you have that particular pet?
3. What was the impact that pet had on you and your life?
4. Finally, how the answers to these questions will improve your life from this day forward?

When we make a choice, it is an insight into ourselves and we need to pay attention. When we make a choice; we change our future. When this occurs, our core values are on display for us and the rest of the world to see.

Core value is a term that gets a lot of use. It is generally described as a principle that guides our internal conduct as well as our relationship with the external world. Most of us don't have a clue what our core values might be. It's said, "A life run on core values has meaning and will benefit the world this life touches." This life is like a bonfire on a cold winter night sending sparks into a starlit sky. Those sparks and that bonfire attract people from all around to congregate, receive its warmth and fellowship with one another.

Like that bonfire and its sparks, a core value driven life is lived from the inside out. It will mean something to you, to others, to the world around you and you will have an impact. The world will be a better place and you will be happy. It doesn't mean it will be perfect or all joy. Even people that are in touch with their core values make mistakes, have miserable spells and aren't universally liked. But, a core value driven life will rebound. It will learn from mistakes, take responsibility, re-focus and strive closer to its goals. Realize that when you look at your pets, you are looking into the reflection of your choices. Your pet selection and that pet's role in your life has meaning. In that meaning, you will find some of your deepest core values. We love these animals. We see ourselves in them and what we love and need the most.

A technique to detect your core values is to listen to yourself when you are angry, if you ever get angry. It may sound like, "It makes me so angry when yada, yada, yada happens." When you cross a core value, you will have an emotional reaction and usually it is anger. For some people, it may be stoicism or going emotionally numb. I know this is pop psychology based on observing you and your pets for decades but it does have merit. Listening to your emotions is constructive for you. Become aware of what makes you angry or numb and you will learn what makes you tick!! It is the best constructive use for anger or stoicism. Emotional reactions build emotional walls that can be difficult to knock down. If you are an angry reactor, the world may see you as a jerk.

Who are the jerks out there? They are the ones who see only their own needs and desires. They never consider others. They are the ones that create stress and fear in others. They are the ones who seek to divide or destroy. They are the ones who hate. They are the ones who abuse. People who abuse pets; abuse people. A child that abuses a pet, or any animal, is a "canary in the mine" for intervention. If you know someone that abuses animals, please, find them some help. Don't wait! Do it now! Take some action! Action is needed for the animal's sake and all the people that this human will injure over the decades.

So, become an advocate for abused animals. Your life and the rest of the world will be better for it. We seldom see true jerks in pets unless there was abuse by the humans in their lives. Rarely, a few animal brains are genetically dysfunctional. Their brains are hypervigilant and see the world as a threat all the time. If you have one of these animals in your life, call your veterinarian for intervention and training advice. Help is available for jerks. It's time to get the jerks out of your life.

A dog's core values might be about food, sleep, sex, territory, or sunny spots. I know that our dachshund, Hannah, will get angry if I cross some of her core values. She won't snap, unless surprised, but she will get irritated, annoyed and angry. I have had Chowchows, Chihuahuas, Sharpeis and Rottweilers, while in my exam room, express to me in no uncertain terms that I am crossing their core values of, "Don't touch me or get into my space. The damage you will incur will be caused by you, not by me. It's nothing personal, you are just crossing my core values."

Now, if I go ahead and cross those core values: the pain, blood and fault are all mine. Most of these breeds know what their core values are and hold tightly to them. You can't beat it out of them, it's very difficult to train it out of them, and you are doing so at your own risk. These traits are very hard-wired into them. Their reactions to having these core values crossed aren't always appropriate. People are injured and dogs are beaten. To a veterinarian and their teams it's never the dog's fault. It's always an uninformed human that causes the issue and no one learns any lessons.

However, for humans, that would be you and me, our core values can be changed. We are flexible. Our brain is malleable or plastic or soft-wired. If a reaction isn't appropriate for the situation, look at why you have reacted, look at the situation and change your mind! People are different. We can change in an instant, in the twinkling of an eye! We don't have to be limited by our genetics. We don't have to be run by that part of our brain where our core values reside. That's the point! We can train ourselves into a more effective and happier Border Collie so we can herd in joy!

Let's cut to the chase. You will have to want to change because you want to. Doing something because you have to, you must, you should or you have no choice, will never make you want to take action. I want my pets wagging their tails and having a good time when they do what I ask. I don't want their ears down, their tail tucked under their belly or having them lie on their backs acting submissive. Are our lives any different? Let's do things for ourselves with an **I want to** motivation, a wagging tail, bright eyes and enthusiasm. Let's get it done by taking action all around!

Vain people (could that be a core value?) are more concerned about how their pet appears to others than their pet's health. Some people will spend a lot more money on grooming their pets than caring for them medically or preventing deadly diseases. This is just my observation but it goes to the core values of, "Why do I have this pet and what does it do for me?" Red is a good example.

Red was just an *old Cocker Spaniel* by many standards. He had smelly ears, a slobbery mouth and was a household fixture more important than the refrigerator. The husband called him the marriage counselor and credited him for keeping their marriage together. Red ran interference with his wife by listening to her conversation so the husband could read the paper in peace. He played with the kids when they got bored and watched over the rug rat as she crawled around the house. When the house became quiet at night, he would sleep on the husband's feet and keep them warm while he digested the latest detective novel. Some evenings, Red would curl up and watch the wife doing her needlepoint. He had a lot of jobs around the house and he was good at them. **Red** was the marriage counselor.

Like Red, our pets play a lot of roles in our lives and they arrive at our doors in unique and sometimes mysterious ways. One common way is that their new pet was adopted from a shelter, a rescue group or may have been found running in the street with no identification, thin and hungry. They may even say that they wanted to save a life. These adopted pets always have interesting names like: Bus Stop –hit by a bus and left in the street, Peg Leg –3 legged cat, Rover –for obvious reasons before he was neutered and many more, some of which I couldn't put in a book. When I ask them how they found their stray, a recycled pet, it sounds a lot like how they found their spouse or significant other. When I point that out to them they will blush, the other will laugh and a core value is exposed. People who find their pets or spouses in that manner are wonderfully caring people.

However, human behavior patterns may be applied in a variety of ways. Mary loved her terrier, Trixie, because it never stopped moving. The spots on Trixie's body were always in motion. She was truly a go-go dog. When Mary came in with her new husband, Ed, I just had to grin. He was a very nice man with all the characteristics of a terrier. He spoke quickly with a lot of animation on his face. He went from window to window in the exam room, read all the posters and thumbed through the dietary display. The squirrels and birds around the feeders seem to catch his eye. He sat briefly when I began to examine Trixie for her semi-annual physical but only long enough to ask questions and to see if he could help. I gently moved his head out of my way so I could see through the otoscope into the ear canal. Mary and her new *Terrier* husband seemed very happy and Trixie had a very compatible new pack member. However you looked at it, Mary now had two 'terriers' in her now very active house and she was happy.

In contrast, I have had many spouses get frustrated because their wife or husband won't give up on a pet. It may be housetraining, behavior or medical issues. This is another example of a core value on display. I usually remind the frustrated spouse that when they get old and grey, their spouse's core value of *not giving up* will be to their own advantage. Their spouse **will not give up** on them either. It's a good thing. We can learn a lot about ourselves in our relationships with our pets.

For me, your pets had an important role in my life. Your pets were your advocates. I learned something about you and your core values when your pets came into our office wagging their tails, confident and happy, well fed (usually too well fed, obesity is the #1 disease of dogs and cats. Oh, gosh, of North American humans too!), with sparkling eyes that would engage me across the waiting room or exam table. These eyes told me you were wonderful people and your pet liked you!

As a young veterinarian, I wasn't sure people had much inherent value. Most of us become veterinarians because we love animals, not people and I was a classic. Early in my career, I had my staff interact with you while I tried to avoid you. I loved your pets. I was sure you were probably a nice person because you had a pet in your life. I didn't want to have a relationship with you, only with your pet. Those attitudes may not sound plausible to you but they existed and do exist in many veterinarians and their teams today. I have recently been teaching in a veterinary technician's program in Canada. In polling my students over the last few years, I can report that you aren't on top of their list, but your pets are. Caring about people takes time.

Over the last 35 years, your pets have taught me about us. It has changed my core values. Your pets taught me to care about you the way they do. Those wagging tails and sparkling eyes said to me, "Don't judge my people. They aren't carbon copies of you. They are wonderful the way they are. Just like me, you need to accept them the way they are. Do it my way and you will see why I love them."

Your pets were correct. In applying their advice about you, I found you to be wonderful creatures. I quit judging your behavior. I looked for the good in you. I began to laugh and enjoy our relationships more fully. When you examine it, we are all just part of a big pack of creatures. The freedom to enjoy you the way you are gave me the freedom to be myself. I didn't have to fit in a role or cater to expectations. I could just be myself and enjoy life. My human relationships became fun for me. I have always been supportive of others and your pets told me that you were ok and that I was ok!! By letting you be you, enjoying you like your pets do, I have learned to enjoy being me. I realized that the greatest gift I could give myself and others was the right to be who we are.

In summary, when you look at your pet listen to what is going on in your mind and heart. Is it about looks? Is it about feelings? Is it about acceptance? Is it about companionship? Is it about filling an empty house with noise? Is it about avoiding the pain humans bring you? Is it about the pleasure your pets brings you? The answers to these questions are reflected back to us when we look at our pets. The answers can change our core values. When we change our core values, we change our life. When we change our life, we change our future. It really is all about you, your future and the love you see reflected in your pet's eyes!

Dr. J'isms

1. Bulldogs, Cockers and Terriers are wonderful creatures.

2. Humans are wonderful creatures.

3. Core values drive our lives and they can be improved!

4. Jerks are jerks.

5. Acceptance is the beginning of joy and fulfillment.

FUN PAGE
In Your Beginning!

1. List 3 reasons why you have or have had any pets. Ex: I wanted a companion or I like taking care of something.

2. List 3 traits that you liked in these pets. Ex: They were happy. They were enthusiastic. They were laid back.

3. Now, list them side-by-side to see how they apply to your life with humans. The traits you like in animals, you will like in humans. Why you select your pets will show you how to select your humans. Now you consciously know some of your core values about your life choices. Wisdom creates healthier choices and a happier life.

Skeeter Loy, herding in all the "right" places!

Chapter 6
Trying To Herd In All The Wrong Places

Wrong, wrong, wrong!! With dogs, as with us, the greatest hindrance to pure joy and unadulterated enthusiasm is being in the wrong place at the wrong time with the wrong activities. There are a lot of clichés in the last sentence, but just think about it. If you take any dog that has genetic behavioral tendencies, such as a Border Collie or an English Pointer and put them in an environment that doesn't validate what they do, they get frustrated and develop behavior problems.

The analogy of a Border Collie living in a city is a valid one. Border Collies are for herding. They were developed as farm machinery, not pets. No matter where you put them, motion activates their brain. They go into their 'zone' with their ears up, their eyes lasered on, their legs snapped out to a wider stance for a quick turning radius and they begin to herd. They don't care what they are herding, they just herd. When the motion doesn't need herding, like a car, bus or train, they get frustrated and can *act out* with behavior that earns them an invalid, "bad dog." Even with good, positive state of the art training, it is difficult to get a Border Collie to adapt to certain environments. Usually, the eventual response is to find them a new home, or have them euthanized because of the "bad dog" behavior. The real issue in these circumstances is that they are just trying to herd in all the wrong places!

Aren't parts of our lives exactly the same way? Any breed of dog, being used within its genetic potential, is happy, well adjusted, enthusiastic and a great companion! Does this last sentence describe you at work and in your relationships? Are you happy, well adjusted, *fired up* and a great companion? Is the world around you a great place to live? Would others describe you that way? Or, in contrast, would you be described as cranky, miserable and herding in all the wrong places. In other words, do those in your world want you to make like snow and flake out of there? They want you to go herd somewhere else! If these last three sentences describe your behavior: Wake up!! If your pet was having behavioral issues, you would want it fixed. Why not fix your own life. Awareness of our own behavior is the beginning of the solution.

The frustration of herding in all the wrong places in humans may be manifested in a whole gamut of negative behaviors and addictions. Hey, mocha latte, anyone, with a little cocaine, meth, sex, sugar or alcohol on the side?

"Last Chance" was the name of the dog that came to our office with issues, besides her name. She woke up snarly, growled if approached and only seemed happy when the owners first came into the house. The fact that their arrival was usually followed by food was the key to Last Chance's happiness. With weeks of work, we realized that good ol' snarly Last Chance just needed a lot more exercise and structure. She needed to be treated like a dog, not a human. She loved working with her people and playing ball. She loved knowing, eventually, that she couldn't get up on the couch or sleep on the foot of the bed. Last Chance survived to an old age in the same, now, happy home.

Our own survival is dependent on the answers that lie within us. These answers have the potential to eliminate our destructive behaviors and addictions. We can find these answers by applying the principle of **herding in all the wrong places**. The key is to look at ourselves and our lives as if we were watching a dog. Not that you are a dog, but looking at you as if your behavior was a dog! If our life doesn't fit us very well and we are miserable living it, we can change it. We can become a happy dog that enjoys all aspects of its life.

Most of us don't know what the answers are because we have never asked the questions. In humans, I have always used the football player analogy. Yes, even women like football! If you were a tackle, being played as a wide receiver or a defensive safety would really frustrate you. You would be too big, too slow and do a lousy job, no matter how hard you wanted or tried to be the best. You would be frustrated, maybe angry and probably develop behavior problems on and off the field. You may drink too much or stay out too late. You make the call!

The cause for this stress and chaos is that you would be, like the Border Collie, trying to herd in all the wrong places. So, the key is to use the genetic strengths of our pets and us to create success. A Border Collie in a blue stem pasture with sheep and a pen is a happy camper and highly successful. This is the kind of success that brings pure, jump out of bed in the morning, all fired up joy! When was the last time you felt like that on a workday! For that matter, when was the last time you felt that way on a vacation day? If we look at our behavior, we can pretty well determine if we are herding in all the right places.

Our pets behavior is hard-wired. It's genetic. To be most successful with our pets we must use their genetic behavioral strengths. Seldom can you train them out of their genetics. However, for us, it's a genetic tendency. While the latest research indicates that our brains are soft-wired. It is a strong tendency but WE can learn to herd wherever we are if we will just get some new training into our brain. All we need to do is create some new brain maps. If we are herding in all the wrong places, maybe we need a new place to herd, maybe we don't. Maybe we need to modify our own behavior and adapt to the new *herding site*.

As an aside, do you know how long you have to do something? The answer is, "Only until you want to do it!" Wanting to or not wanting to is always a choice. Sure, that's easy for me to say because it's not my life, my stresses or my disasters. However, most of us don't realize that we can change our behavior and currently live our lives by 'default'. Come on, no matter how old you are, don't you think it's time for you to be in charge of your own behavior by training your brain and creating the life you want?

Being in charge of your life will be interesting and different, won't it? I had clients whose animals were in charge of their owner's lives. We all joke about our pets letting us live with them, but John and Beth had a three month old, blue eyed, white ball of fluff as a new kitten in their home. After a week or so, they called in a panic from their bedroom phone. This sweet little ball of fur, hiss, teeth and claws wouldn't let them down the hall of their home. They were pinned in their bedroom!! Don't laugh. It happened and they weren't laughing! Well, maybe you can laugh a little because it happened to someone else. We used distraction techniques with their kitten to enable them to escape from their bedroom and get to work. On examination, I found that the kitten was deaf from birth and had some issues that needed unique training. It took some work on their part, but they got to keep the kitten. However, its name changed from Fluffy to Jaws! Hand signals and rewards changed all of their lives. Some clients are abused by or allow their pets or children to be in charge of their lives. Truly! Who is in charge of yours?

Another husband and wife team rescued a dog that had a few issues. When bedtime came, George would growl and threaten them until they started to go to bed. George determined when bedtime in their home was. He was a true drill instructor. The good news is that even drill instructors respond to new training. For these clients, when daylight savings time hit, their bedtime changed! Something similar is when clients allow their pet to sleep with Mum and Dad. Some of these pets will growl or snap when Mum or Dad accidentally touches the other while sleeping! It can make for an exciting middle-of-the-night crisis! I love dogs and cats but we should be running their lives instead of them running ours. And, maybe we should be running our own lives or even our children's lives.

We all know that the only control we have in our lives is how we react to what life brings our way. It's that old "life happens" stuff. Controlling our lives is about us and not about others. So, when life does happen, what are you going to do about it? Animals usually take some kind of action. They react immediately in some manner. Humans usually procrastinate, suffer or take it out on others. The time for change is Now! Training our Border Collie brains to do what we want will increase our happiness, fulfillment and success. Learning to herd in all the right places is about learning our genetic behavioral strengths and then training them to be used in the right environment. If you aren't "all fired up," then you need to look at where you are herding! The answers lie inside of you!

Dr. J'isms

1. Success is herding in all the right places

2. Success is changing where we herd if it's the wrong place.

3. Success is what happens after "life happens".

4. An English Pointer should be pointing Quail, not dumpsters.

5. A Border Collie shouldn't be herding taxis.

6. Pets teach us about ourselves only if we pay attention!

FUN PAGE
Herding In All Your Right Places

1. List 3 things you absolutely detest doing.

   a. Think about and write down how you can change your behavior so you will never have to do them again.

2. List 3 things you absolutely love to do.

   a. Figure out and write down how you can change your behavior so you can do them all the time.

3. List 3 things you like to do but that are difficult for you.

   a. Figure out how you can change your behavior so you can enjoy doing the difficult things and write them down.

Hannah, ready to watch some football?

Chapter 7
Football, Baby ... Bring It!

If you enjoy what you are doing, but the environment doesn't match your joy, change it. If what you are doing is just plain bad for you, then change it. Changing it is a simple concept that is harder to apply. To what or why or where you would change it? We stay connected to jobs, relationships, activities or habits (good or bad) because we don't think we have any alternatives that are appealing. It is self-protective to dislike change and as a result, we just go along with what we are going along with. It's like the story about the farmer that has a hound dog lying on his front porch moaning. The visitor asks the farmer why the dog seems to be in pain. The farmer answers, "He,s lying on a nail." The visitor asks, "Why doesn't he get up and move?" The farmer answers: "I guess the nail just isn't in far enough." We have all heard that story and it does make a point (so to speak).

Pain is relative and personal. Sometimes, the perception of the pain of change is greater than the real pain of the 'nail' we are lying on. You already know that the reality is we get to choose our pain of preference. Don't we live the life we have because it seems to be the least painful choice rather than the most joyful?

Animals are similar. The same procedure, such as a vaccination, used on a variety of breeds, elicits very different responses. Some act as if nothing has occurred. A Bichon Friese reacts with an Academy Award performance. I know I'm generalizing, but this breed can be one of the most dramatic in the world of dogs. They are the actors of the dog world. There is no stoicism. They just don't sit there and take it. They are not biters or snappers, but they are screamers! Clients with patients waiting elsewhere in the building are certain someone is getting beaten.

Even knowing it's a performance, I always felt guilty. Bichon's may have a breed difference such as a lower threshold for pain. However, personally, I've found that as I age, my nerves don't conduct pain as efficiently. When I was a younger veterinarian in my 20's, any wound would screamingly hurt. Now, in my 60's I find my wounds when my blood is splattering around the exam room. At least it hurts less now than then!

All humans and animals have genetic 'hard wired' strengths or brain tendencies. You are a Border Collie because we have Border Collie brains that contain our strengths. Where we differ is that we have higher centers in our brain that can *control* or *train* the Border Collie part of our brain. This relationship in our own head is the same relationship that we have with our pets. In our heads, we have a 'dog trainer', the executive center and a 'dog', our reptilian brain. We can train our Border Collie brains. To change our behavior, it is easiest to go with our strengths, our "hard-wired" strengths.

Let's go back to our football analogy. Football players are jokingly known to be "animals" and require training to be effective. How is that different than your pet or your brain?

We have discussed that an offensive tackle is happiest when he is on the playing field, in the line, ready to block, on count, on the attack ... moving toward winning the game, with the team, with his strengths! Nothing feels better to an offensive tackle than a pancake block or watching the running back blast by him and down the field. Our lives can have that same blast of enthusiasm. We want to be on the winning team. We want to be on the attack with a certainty that what we are doing has impact. It's our future! It's what fires us up. Tomorrow is the first morning of your future!! Bounce out like you are a dog ready for breakfast!

Think about a pet's response when you get the leash out or start the can opener or get out of your chair near dinner time. If you look into their eyes, you will see, "Oh, boy, here we go!! Da human is ready to do something!! Wow, what will it be?! Yes, it's the leash!! That leash is attached to so many good smells, such visual vistas and such fun!! Spin, spin, bounce, bounce, bark, bark (SSBBBB) let the human know that this is a great, read that as a great idea!!" Exuberance abounds, even in old dogs that can hardly move!

When was the last time you thought about your life, or your job (you know, just over broke!) or your career or your relationships or your habits with that look in your eye. That look is a reflection of the SSBBBB attitude about your day? If not, why not? How do our pets do that and how can we get there in our lives. Few of us have the joy we see in our pets, but we can.

Our goal is to find that deep fire within us that we have almost smothered, crushed, put on hold, nearly lost. But if it's in our pets, it's still in us! It's a fire that never dies. The furnace may be off, but the pilot light is still burning! All we need to do is turn the thermostat to a new level.

Some of you may be saying or thinking, "But you don't know what I've been through! You don't know how hard it is. You don't know where I am in life. You must have had some advantages. Life will never be the same. (Life is never the same because life happens every day!) I'm too afraid to make the change. I think I'll just play it safe."

I can't argue with any of these statements or the hundreds of others we can all make. However, when you look into the eyes of your pet, consider what you want. Topics like these are some of the things we will look at during this short sojourn into the world of you and your pets. Even as I write this, our dachshund Hannah is curled up into a ball in her bed on the floor next to me. She is contented, sleeping and snoring, while she waits for us to go to bed. When we head for bed, only then she can go to her proper bed in our bedroom. Life is tough for our pets, eh? While our world is more complicated theirs, it can be as simple as making it what we want, instead of what we have! Will it be easy? Probably not. Will it be worthwhile? Only the future knows that answer. Do you hear an emotion in the last few paragraphs or is it only the wind whispering in the trees? The future is ours to take. Let's do it!

Dr. J'isms

1. If your life doesn't match what you want: Change it!

2. If you aren't happy: Change your life!

3. If you can't change your life: Adapt!

4. If you can't adapt: get used to being miserable!

5. If being miserable doesn't make you happy: Tough!

6. If you think you can't choose: You have chosen!

7. If you don't like your choice today: Choose differently tomorrow!

FUN PAGE
Football? You Pick Your Game

1. Pick 3 situations at work or in life that you avoid and write them down.

    a. Decide on a solution for each and then do it.

2. Pick 3 careers you would rather be doing, qualified or not.

    a. Make two lists. Why you can and why you can't. Throw away the *why you can't* list.

3. Pick 3 activities you want to do but don't. Ex: draw, paint, exercise.

    a. Do each one for 15 minutes today ... today!

Todger in an *all fired up* frame of mind.

Chapter 8
All Fired Up (S.s.b.b.b.b.) Or Dying

There are only two stages of life. Count 'em! Two, and only two! You are either "all fired up" or you are "just waiting to die!" It was your pets that taught me this.

The all fired up thing has to do with that "spin, spin, bounce, bounce, bark, bark" (S.S.B.B.B.B.) canine enthusiasm in our own lives, work, projects and relationships. I don't care what you see in life to S.S.B.B.B.B. about, as long as you see something. Our pets certainly do, even if it's only the Post person at the door or a sunny spot on the floor.

Most of the time, our fears, our lack of knowledge about our strengths, the judgments of others or being trained from birth that we have no strengths hinders our S.S.B.B.B.B. This doesn't just slow us down, it slams the door on our fingers. It just hurts too much to even try! This is true whether we are 10, 20 or 90 years old.

Our pets live in S.S.B.B.B.B. daily, but do we? They don't reach the 'just waiting to die' part of life until the very 'brick wall' end of their physiological lives. Their bodies are breaking down, toxins are flooding their systems and they, if they had their choice, would crawl away and disappear. As a veterinarian, I can see this stage in their eyes. They just have 'the look.' They are tired and worn out. The light has dimmed in their eyes and they move sluggishly, if they move at all. It's the sad time for us, but they're just finished. They are too pooped to pop, their give a damn is busted! And you, if it's your pet, will hit a point where you know in your heart that the end is near.

Stunningly, in humans, you can see "the look" in many people's eyes when they are in their teens, 20's, 30's and in all stages and ages of life. If you haven't looked into the mirror lately, take the time to look into your eyes and see what 'look' you have. You don't have to be afraid, just turn on the light and look in the mirror. It's only you standing there. People look into your eyes all the time. Most of them like what they see. Your pets always like what they see. Quick, stop reading and go look in a mirror. If you don't find the s.s.b.b.b.b. all fired up look, it leaves only the 'just waiting to die' look, so look closely. These are the only two phases of life.

Don't tell me what you have seen, tell yourself what you see. If you aren't sure what you see, pick up your pet and look at both of you in the mirror. What do you see? If your look is different than your pets, you need some work! Our pets primarily live in the 'all fired up' stage. Fortunately for us, a transitional training period can change our 'look!' Now is the time to take action!

Ask yourself this question. Would the world around you be changed if you were gone? I'll refer to this later, but are you having an impact on life or is life just having an impact on you? Is life beating you up or are you going to be in that S.S.B.B.B.B. mode until your body wears out?

The key to the future, for us, is through the attitudes that we see expressed in our pets. These attitudes will take you where you want to go if you spend some time doing what your pet does: Stop, look, listen and S.S.B.B.B.B.! If you don't find what you want, if you don't know what you want, then start looking and changing. We are in charge of our lives, not our Border Collie brains. Go get 'em!

Dr. J'isms

1. "The look" we see in the mirror shows what we have today!

2. What we see tomorrow in the mirror is up to us!

3. Are we living all fired up or waiting to die?

4. We choose, we choose, we choose!

5. Let's cut to the chase. We choose!

6. We see today what we have chosen!

7. We will see tomorrow what we choose today!

FUN PAGE
Are You S.S.B.B.B.B. OR DEAD?

1. List 3 things that fire you up in good ways and 3 things that hinder you.

    a. Do the good things over and over.

    b. Stop the *hindering* things now.

2. Go to a mirror, check your 'look' and then make faces.

    a. See how a happy S.S.B.B.B.B. face changes your 'look'.

    b. See how a sad and angry faces change your 'look'.

    c. Stop the sad and angry faces now.

3. Choose to do 3 things you have been avoiding at home.

    a. Do one with the S.S.B.B.B.B. attitude.

    b. Do one with a sad and angry face.

    c. Choose a. or b. for your third task and your future.

Joss and Hannah sleeping during a Kansas Dog Day afternoon

Chapter 9
Strengths And Change

Hey, Beagles 'sniff', Border Collies 'herd', Retrievers 'retrieve' and Pointers 'point'! These are genetic 'hard-wired' behavioral strengths. This is the stuff they are born with. To use these breeds most effectively and to create a well-adjusted, happy dog, you want to use their genetic tendencies to aid you and let them be all they can be!

How about us? Would that apply to us? Let's talk about dog behavior that I have observed over the decades. Let's talk about how we are no different in our genetic behavioral tendencies. I'm warning you in advance that this section will be a lot of fun, create some thought for you and have some action attached to it. You will begin to realize your strengths as we go through this. Applying and training those strengths is the hard part … the action part!

For a veterinarian there are no ugly dogs and there are no ugly hard-wired strengths! There is no good or bad … everything is just different. What is just is! Unused strengths are the same as having none. Turning weaknesses into strengths is a different topic. But for now, why would I use a Chihuahua to guard my business at night? Huh? Chihuahuas are wonderful creatures and can guard your chair in your home and defend it with great ferociousness until you come back from the refrigerator, but that's about it.

Identifying your behavioral strengths, then acting on them is where benefit, change and the future you design meet the road. Hard-wired strengths carried to the extreme under stress have a negative effect, but under control, they are the driving force for your life. These strengths are your potential waiting to be put to use. Think about it, if you are a *Hummer* and drive yourself onto a go-cart track … what you will create is chaos, anger, a lot of damaged go-carts and waste your *Hummer's* potential. However, a well running go-cart on a go-cart track life can be a lot of fun and have a lot of success! Doggie D.I.S.C. is coming up soon, so pay attention!

Clients have asked me over the years whether or not they should we get another dog for their aging dog? First, I ask them if they want another dog in their home. What they want is critical.

Here is a short diversion. The, "What do you want?" question is also critical to our brain function. When we ask the, "What do you want? What do I want?" question, we are asking the question most people don't ask themselves. The answer to this question is a major key to success. The *what do you want* mentality jump-starts our brain into an action mode. That question is the can opener in your dog or cat's life!

All you have to do to see the impact on your dog is to say, "Hannah - do you want dinner?" Bang, a flurry of feet and instant action from Hannah! The same applies to our brains and to us. It creates motivation to get off our fannies and do something. It creates action. Now, let's get back to getting a new pet for an older dog or cat!

Secondly, because of the pack mentality, older dogs (most of them) will accept a puppy, but rarely an adult dog (it's that territorial thing, same as in humans) unless it has lived with another dog during its life. An older dog can help the newbie with housetraining and other training, both good and not so good! (We'll have another Joss story soon). I tell clients that dogs love us. To them I'm convinced that we are just funny looking dogs that don't speak dog very well. We are a part of their pack and they accept us as we are.

As funny looking dogs, they understand that we don't speak dog very well, so they have to learn our language, our way of doing things and adapt to our schedule. The analogy would be that if you speak only English and go to a country where they speak only Spanish, Japanese, Russian or German communication is tough. That is the way it is with our dogs. So, while our pets do love us, they really, really love another dog! Real dogs speak their language, move the correct way, love to play and understand all the nuances of dog communication. Most of this is body language, just as in humans. So bringing in another dog, especially a puppy, actually enhances and extends an older dog's life.

When a puppy comes into the house, initially older dogs are a little irritated. As long as they don't attempt to attack and kill the newcomer, they will work out a good relationship. Rarely do they avoid them full time, forever.

But, in the beginning, they seem to think, "Darn it, life was so set up, so predicable, so comfortable and now they bring this thing into my space. Snort, if I just ignore it for a few days, maybe it'll go away!" This is just like our approach to changes in our lives. These can be changes in our relationships with co-workers, bosses, family, friends, our health status and any other change that occurs. The key for our lives is found in how the older dog begins to adapt to the new dog in the home. If it doesn't try to kill the new pet, the older dog appears to start to think like this, "Okay, this thing is bugging me but it behaves like a dog, it kind of looks like a dog, it talks like a dog, maybe it wouldn't be so bad if it had some training!"

Then relationships begin to happen, expand and everyone gets on the same page, eventually. The older dog now has something to get up for in the morning, someone to share the sunny spot with, some one to interact with all the time. Suddenly, the older dog has a responsibility, a reason for living and will find a new level of all fired up motivation! Increased movement makes the arthritis feel better, increased aggravation decreases sleep patterns and suddenly life is seen through another dog's eyes.

Life events like, "You silly little dog, you won't catch that butterfly, or that squirrel, especially that squirrel. Hey, that's rabbit poop, not food! Look out, that's the edge of the deck … whoops, crash and burn! Boy, could I teach him or her a few things!" The old smells seem new again! Like us, older dogs don't like change. A new puppy isn't a blessed event for them in the beginning. Change for us is seldom seen as a blessed event. However, once they adjust, it increases their life span, improves the quality of their later years, and helps them focus on things other than *waiting to die* topics. Oops, I have slipped into human behavior and attitudes again. I could say I'm sorry, but I'm not!

Any new thing in our lives, whether by force or choice, is similar to what you just read about in the last paragraphs. It doesn't have to be a new puppy or a new human. It could be a job or career change. It could be a defining moment in your life, after which, nothing is ever the same. It could be the death of a close friend or a family member. It could be a minor or major change in health status. It could be any new thing. The impact on us is the same as the impact of that puppy on an older dog. Nothing is ever the same after that event. It doesn't mean it is good or bad. It is only different. Whoa! Let's see, the only thing guaranteed in life is what? Change. The only control we have in life is how we respond to what happens? Life happens? Does it happen only to you?

Should we get **all fired up** and train our brain to adapt to change or just hope it will go away and continue waiting to die? Who makes these choices? The defining message we get from our pets is very simple. Sunny spot or shade, floor or lap, my bed or their bed? Make a choice! Then, do it! Go to the sunny spot or shade, the floor or lap, one bed or the other! Action, action, action! If you don't like it, then take a new action, action, action!

Finally, another quick Joss and Hannah story. Joss, our Border Collie, was with us first. Joss was the brightest, sweetest, most enthusiastic piece of farm machinery you could ever have known. She really wanted to please us and behave as farm machinery, of course. A few years later, an older client, knowing I have been a lifelong Dachshund fan, gave me a 6 month old Dachshund puppy that she had purchased, couldn't train and because her living circumstances had changed meant that she couldn't keep her any longer. My wife wasn't too enamored with the idea in the beginning. She had never been around Dachshunds and wasn't sure she wanted two dogs, since Joss was really well adjusted, housetrained, and nothing but a joy.

Hannah came thundering into our home wanting to play. She was a social dog with a go, go, go, go, go attitude. She would bounce over to Joss, jump into her face, pull on her ears and fur, run around her and bark at her. Hannah was a truly S.S.B.B.B.B. type of dog.

It took us a few days to realize that Joss was now living in doggie hell and we had created it. She was very sweet, but she didn't know how to react to this thing we brought into her life.

Joss's life had changed, and she couldn't tell how to react. Like many of us with our own changes, she didn't know what to do. In fact, when Hannah would start her S.S.B.B.B.B. thing, Joss would almost go catatonic. She would freeze into a sitting or standing position. The only thing that would move were her eyes and they were usually looking at us with a silent plea for help. Her stress was evident to us, but not to Hannah! Hannah was just having fun with her new toy whose name was Joss. Joss was about 35 pounds of farm equipment and Hannah was about 8 pounds of self-centered, fun-loving, bull-headed, S.S.B.B.B.B. Dachshund. Joss would have had other descriptive terms for Hannah, I'm sure. Never did Joss attempt to bite Hannah or harm her in any way. It took us weeks to get Hannah house trained. Ok, I lie. Actually, it took my wife a few weeks to get Hannah housetrained and to help Joss adjust to the moving, snapping, tugging and barking change in her life.

Joss and Hannah became the best of friends. Joss and Hannah became the best kind of friends. It did take some time. It took patience. It took persistence. It took consistency. Finally, it took training. A lot of training was require, but the results were outstanding.

All of these descriptive terms, patience, persistence, consistent, and outstanding describe my wife! There is something about the Canadian Scottish sense of what is right is right, what is just is just and if it applies to one, it should apply to all. While Hannah was bullheaded, Sondra was analytically determined. Determined always trumps bullheadedness!

Even so, when change occurs in our own lives, our brains can be as equally bullheaded as Hannah. If we do what we did with the Joss-Hannah situation by applying patience, persistence and consistency with determination through training, the results can be equally outstanding! If we want, or must, have change in our own lives, the same standards apply. We must train our brain by using patience, persistence and consistency with determination to create an outstanding success story! I'm looking forward to hearing your success story!

Dr. J'isms

1. Change chosen or forced: Never welcome!

2. Adaptation creates benefit!

3. Chosen adaptation creates success!

4. Adaptation without desire creates a rut!

5. Change chosen or forced: Creates heaven or hell!

6. Good news: It's our heaven or hell!

FUN PAGE
Your Strengths And Change

1. List 3 new things you love to do and why. These are strengths.

2. List 3 changes in your life in the last month that you have resisted.

3. Put list 1 and 2 side by side and see how list 1 helps you adjust to list 2.

From http://www.petexpertise.com/dog-bell-training.html

Chapter 10
Bell Training Hannah, Joss And Ourselves

Success in housetraining Hannah occurred because of a technique my mother used to train our Dachshunds when we were kids. Remember, Dachshunds are bullheadedness on a leash. Undisciplined bullheadedness is the worst kind of bullheadedness. Mom mentioned how she trained our Dachshunds to my wife when Hannah was being so, uh, resistant, and she used it to housetrain Hannah quickly.

Since then, I have recommended it to my clients. She tied a bell, one big enough to hear around the house, to a string on the back doorknob (or wherever your pooping door is) and rang it with Hannah's paw or nose when they went out. Hannah liked this game and quickly learned it! As you can imagine, she soon became a tyrant, ringing the bell to go out anytime, for anything she wanted. She would look through the sliding door on the deck and see the squirrel, the neighbor's cat, the birds or the mice and would thunder through the house to the bell. However, tyrant or not, she 'got it' and was housetrained!

Hannah's natural exuberance made her bell ringing exuberant! Whang, bing, bing, bing, bing, bing! She would whang it off the door, the dryer, a wall, anything that bell could reach! Then Hannah's head would peer around the corner into the hall to see who was coming to fulfill her immediate "Hellooooo, I'm here, what are you waiting for, let's goooo!" demands. If her request was urgent, she would kick her exuberance into a higher gear. Then there would be more whanging and more peering down the hall!

The bell training worked so well because it made her the center of attention and it was fun! It got an immediate, action oriented response from us. In the beginning of the bell whanging, we ran to validate her behavior. For Hannah, because of her personality, her training has always had to be fun and action oriented. You'll understand this when we get to the Doggie DISC chapter. Everything with Hannah was going well. We had no more anointed carpeting and we didn't have to spend a lot of time watching to make sure we weren't missing any clues. Trust existed again in our lives. Life was settling down.

Then, one evening, while working in our office near the bell door, I heard a very tiny tinkle, tinkle, sound of a bell. So soft, that even though I was only 10 feet away in the next room, I wasn't sure I heard it. Then, there it was again, with a very small, very tentative, very tinkle, tinkle with small t's sound. It was a "Excuse me, I don't want to impose and I'm not sure I'm supposed to do this but could you help me, maybe? Please?" kind of bell sound. I walked into the hall and there stood Joss, this piece of intelligent, confident, focused farm machinery with a kind of head down guilty look on her face. She had rung the bell, sort of. She wasn't sure it was okay and she didn't want to impose at all, but she figured that if it worked for Hannah, then she would give it a try!

Joss, being a very smart dog, figured that one out on her own. The difference in their bell ringing technique is what brings us to finding our own strengths in "Doggie D.I.S.C.!" With Joss and Hannah, their genetic hard-wired behavioral tendencies were reflected in their bell technique throughout their lives. It only our ears to know who wanted out!

Dr. J'isms

1. If *things* aren't working, try a new way.

2. Most goals can be accomplished in a variety of ways.

3. An *old* way could be the newest 'new' way.

4. Learning from others is the least painful way.

5. Your way is the best way for you!

FUN PAGE
Your Bell Training

1. List 3 things that aren't working well in your life.

2. Pretend that items on list 1 are dogs that need training. Give them a name.

3. Since they are now dogs, list at least 2 ways to change the results of each item in 1.

Dickon: a C/S

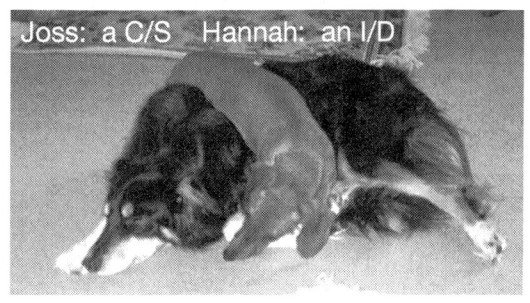

Pippin: an I/S
Tucker: an S/C

Todger: a D/C

Khalifah: an S/I

Joss: a C/S   Hannah: an I/D

Chapter 11
Doggie D-I-S-C

The DISC model of human behavior applies to all mammals. This chapter will explain in "cut to the chase" terms how to identify some of your strengths and to understand the behavior of all the animals in your life, even the two-legged ones!

Forget the details in this book, there aren't many. I have by style and intent made this an instruction manual that is fairly blunt. It's this veterinarian's take on life. This chapter is about the patented model of human behavior called D.I.S.C. Its primary purpose, in my opinion, is to identify genetically based, hard wired behavioral tendencies or strengths. It's found in that Border Collie or reptilian and midbrain part of your brain.

This is why Border Collies herd, Retrievers retrieve, Beagles and Bassett hounds sniff and so on. This system has been around since the 1920's of years but was statistically validated in the 1980's. It is a sound way to evaluate human behavioral strengths. In these strengths, there are no good or bad, better or worse strengths, only different. Each blend brings an asset to the world.

When understood and applied, D.I.S.C. creates dramatically better communication, relationships and self-esteem. This model can be applied to all mammals but we're going to look at it as it applies to dogs and learn something about ourselves. My wife and I are advanced certified human behavior consultants through Personality Insights, Inc. of Atlanta. The knowledge this system imparts is simple and easily applied in learning about individual behavioral strengths and the emotions that go with them. When we focus on our strengths, life goes better! When we know our strengths, we can focus our brain training more effectively. When we apply it to our pets and the people around us life becomes a lot more fun.

Start thinking about the pets you have known and how they behaved. They all behaved a little differently, just like us, even though they were all dogs. In this section, we'll look at them through 8 parameters. I apologize, again, because this isn't an in-depth study and is pretty much "cut to the chase." The information is a lot of fun and easily understood. It helps you understand you and your pet's behavior. It has some detail, so make notes if you want! For more info: www.bordercolliebrain.com

First, are they outgoing or reserved? Joss was much more

reserved (eye contact and a slow tail wag), while Hannah was outgoing (S.S.B.B.B.B.)! Now, think about your pets: calm and quiet or loud and active? How about yourself? Are you more reserved or more outgoing? Are you more like Joss? Are you more like Hannah? Joss was content to do things by herself, while Hannah was like a people magnet. She would stick to people wherever they were and had to be with them!

"MOTOR" ACTIVITY

OUTGOING
RESERVED

Reserved dogs are quieter. It takes more to get them wound up and excited. When they notice you, they wag their tail slowly. If you approach them, they will back up, turn sideways and might avoid intense eye contact. They bark less frequently and only when they are making a point and only because they have to. They don't bark just to hear themselves bark! They aren't in your lap, bouncing all around you and being, well, sort of nuts. They are great companions to snuggle up with on a sofa while you read. They love to do things with you but won't usually bug you with 'their thing' all the time. They don't have to be the center of attention. If they are stressed or out of control, they will be very submissive, avoiding confrontations and may anoint the floor, carpet and furniture with yellow. If they are male, they may become an upside down fountain of yellow!

Outgoing dogs are much more active, wanting to do 'their' thing. Their tail wags quickly; barking (talking) is more prevalent. They are much more 'in your face' about things, more demanding, more energetic, just more, more, more! These are high energy dogs. They love to do 'active' things, then just crash and burn. Many are either going or sleeping, on or off!

Think about your pets, current or past, and see which behaviors they fall into. However, like us, they exhibit some of each, but they fall into one category or the other most of the time, just like you! If you have ever thought: "Oh, just give me a break." Then you have an outgoing dog. If they are out of control, you will think: My dog must have A.D.H.D.!"

Jack Russell Terriers, while wonderful dogs, are a breed that behaves in the A.D.H.D. mode. Bichon Frieses, as I said earlier, are the actors of the dog world. They are such drama queens!

Here is another point I'll mention several times: A genetic behavioral strength or that hard-wired tendency carried to an extreme becomes a weakness and creates stress. We can use this information to make our life with our pets more complete and fun. Even as we can use this information to make our life and relationships with the rest of the world more complete and fun!

Generally, breeds of dogs will have tendencies toward a certain style of behavior but within the breed, you will find all the parameters present, so don't be misled. However, when looking for a breed of dog, the Doggie D.I.S.C. system will help you select what you want. Your veterinarian is a good resource for information about breeds and their behavioral tendencies. Your own desires are much more important. It is easier to train a more reserved dog than an outgoing one, but much easier to train an intelligent dog than one that isn't so bright. All dogs are trainable except with that very rare exception whose brains are truly defective. We'll talk about selecting pets later.

All right, so, more reserved or more outgoing. Write down two lines, one going horizontally and put 'outgoing' above and 'reserved' below. I know, get a piece of paper and do it … sit, heel, stay! It's a task! Now, put a vertical line through the middle of the horizontal line…it should look like a '+'.

Secondly, are they *task* or *people*'oriented? This is the left and right side of the D.I.S.C. model as you look at it on the page. The left side is the task side. The right side is the people side. Put a circle around all

"COMPASS" ACTIVITY

TASK ← → PEOPLE

of it. So we have four quadrants with the upper two being more outgoing, the lower two being more reserved, the left two being more task oriented, the right two more people oriented. This is the D.I.S.C. model seen earlier in this chapter.

Task oriented dogs are much more interested in working. They are always fulfilling their genetics rather than interacting with you. Much of their work may involve you but when on a walk with a Beagle, for example, it may wander away by itself, doing its thing following the scent in its nose and then an hour later, suddenly look up and wonder, "Now where did they go?" The walk was a very enjoyable task. You were incidental!

For Task oriented dogs (left side of the D.I.S.C. model) their fulfillment, their play, their joy, is 'doing what comes naturally' (or genetically). Most humans that are similarly task oriented see their world in the same manner. Anything that isn't a 'task' is boring, has no purpose and is a waste of time! That includes people. They get along with people but would rather do their own thing without other people involvement. Social interaction is incidental. It isn't necessary for their life to be full.

That was part of Joss' problem with Hannah. Joss was a reserved/task oriented dog and Hannah, being outgoing/people oriented, only wanted to play, have fun and interact: "Come on, Joss, let's boogie down!" Joss didn't have a clue what 'boogie down' meant or how to respond to all that energy. Does that sound like your pets? Perhaps it is some of your co-workers or maybe even you? Give a task oriented, dog or human, a task and they are in hog heaven! Whatever that is! Ask them to go party and you can expect some form of rejection!

For People oriented dogs (right side of the D.I.S.C. model) their fulfillment, their play and their joy is having someone to interact with. They need an animal or, in us, a people fix frequently. You put them in a room by themselves with a task and they aren't happy campers. They literally need some creature contact to feel normal. The world is out of synch; the stars aren't lined up correctly; something is just wrong if there are no other creatures around to interact with. No people in their presence (or other dogs) will create a huge conflict for them.

Some destructive behavior in dogs (and people?) is related to this type of behavioral tendency. I won't get into details of negative behavior but if that 'separation anxiety syndrome' occurs in your pet or friends or co-workers or children or spouse?, looking at some of these issues will help resolve it. These people oriented creatures are the easiest to relate to. They really do love people. People are their lifeblood. Tasks: who cares? Let's have some fun or help someone out.

In review, above the line is outgoing, below is reserved, left is task, right is people, with a circle around it all. That leaves four categories and is where the D.I.S.C. comes in. Upper left is D. Upper right is I. Lower right is S. Lower left is C. So you have D/I above, C/S below. You have D/C left and I/S right. All creatures (including humans) are hard-wired to function primarily out of one area with another as a lesser or supportive trait and usually, they are adjacent to each other, such as being a D/I, or an S/C or a C/S. Small percentages of the population have more than two traits dominating, such as I/D/C or have cross over traits, such as an S/D or an I/C.

These traits are not better or worse, just different. These traits are not good or bad (unless out of control creating stress), just different. In life, all four of these traits will be used at times. Under stress an I/D for example, will go from his or her I trait to a D. Some people have found that this explains why they (or their child/spouse/pet) acted so differently when under stress compared to normal.

We will look at all four D/I/S/C areas and then at some examples. If you want better relationships, better communication, a more joyful lifestyle, a better work environment and to enjoy your dog, cat, child, spouse, co-workers, or the world in general more fully, the next pages will bring you enlightenment. You can build relationships that last and your stress with people will decrease.

This isn't 'warm and fuzzy clap trap,' this is science based and one way to a better quality life for you and your pet! The analogy I use is that I communicate in English. I could speak a little Spanish if I needed but I usually communicate in English. If you speak a different language than I do, communication is difficult. Knowing each other's *language* makes life a lot easier, more efficient and less stressful. The way we behave is the major part of communication.

We use a behavioral style that is a reflection of who we are. It reflects our genetically *hard-wired* style. Knowing how to *read* other people's style and *communicate* in their style is a key to success. It's the way we are all wired. Dogs and humans are hard-wired in similar ways. Here comes Doggie D.I.S.C.!

The D behavioral style

These dogs and humans are task oriented with action and are very outgoing. He/she (notice, it's not a gender thing) may appear friendly, but when approached, they growl or bark. They are more apt to approach you in some manner. D's like a challenge and can be challenging.

Making direct eye contact with a D, regardless of species, is a challenge to them and they will react. If you do make eye contact with a D, don't wimp out and look away first. Being a wimp will put you lower in the pack and can create relationship problems unless you like being a wimp and lower in the pack. If you do make eye contact, create a distraction, such as moving your hand or talk, use "good dog" or anything that causes them to break eye contact first! D's don't respect anyone that backs down. They don't forget.

D's don't mind equals but they will challenge superiors and can attack wimps. Good behavior training is critical in D's, dog or human, at a very early age. If they get bored, they will create a challenge. Destructive behavior, for example, is creating a challenge. D's have to be treated as if they are dogs (especially human D's). They must be well trained in basic obedience and always given choices. If a D dog is allowed to sleep with you, curl up on the couch with you, sit in your lap, eat off your plate or drink from your glass they could decide that they are in charge of the pack. I have met many Chihuahua's who are in charge in their homes! Size or gender does not make a D!

All of the behavior parameters, in my opinion, apply to all species. However, some breeds are predisposed to increased frequency of certain types. Your veterinarian can help you with these breed tendencies. You are on your own with the humans in your life, but if you apply these techniques to people you meet and know, your relationships and understanding of how others function in the world will make your life a lot happier.

When D's are in charge, they will treat you like any pack member. With dog D's, since we don't speak dog very well, we see their behavior as aggressive and unpredictable. They may appear prickly and intense. If we let it go on long enough, we will have a problem. If these dogs have an emotional response, it is usually anger or aggression. Making these dogs work is one way to maintain control. They like action. They like tasks. A tired D is usually a more manageable D. Basic obedience works: Come, sit, down, stay, heel, shake a paw and roll over with you in charge helps.

Using work, such as this, reinforces that you are the pack leader. As humans, we need to have the same attitude toward our Border Collie brains. We are the pack leader in our head, not our genetics! Training our brains is the key factor to a happy, successful life. Training our brains to use our genetic tendencies to their fullest extent or adapting them to what we want in life is what success is all about!

The I behavioral style

These dogs (and humans) are more outgoing and people oriented. The I is in the upper right quadrant of D.I.S.C. model. These are the most outgoing dogs. They love everybody! They are the most active. They have energy beyond belief! They are the truly active... party, party dogs. Everything has to be fun! This is really how they see life. Life is a party with places to go, things to do and people to see. Social isolation is a bummer. They hate to be alone, period. They bark or *talk* more, they want to be with you, they want to be in your lap, under your feet, cooking with you in the kitchen and will follow you around the house wherever you are going to be ... just in case a party breaks out!

Humans love I dogs, but not all dogs do. For many dogs, the I dog is too active, too pushy, too noisy and too wiggly. Human I types fall into the same categories for many humans. If you don't have I in play as a part of your style,

I's can seem a little over the top. They aren't, they just seem that way! I's love to be stars, the center of attention. When the I dog arrives in your life, your life just lights up! Everything is better with them around, life is more exciting, life is a lot more fun with the I around ... dog or human! It may not be so productive but it's a lot more fun!

Training the I style must involve fun of some kind. They are worried about being liked and severe discipline can break their spirit and create behavior problems. Again, basic obedience, while it may look like work, can be fun for the I dog and help them structure their natural enthusiasm! Human I's need structure to be effective. Humans with high I tendencies become successful when they learn how to make lists and work from them. When you have the S.S.B.B.B.B. (spin/spin/bounce/bounce/bark/bark) dog or human at home, they are almost always an I type.

The S behavioral style

These dogs and humans are more reserved, and care about people. This takes us to the lower right quadrant of the D.I.S.C. model. The S type of dog wags their tail more slowly and they break eye contact quicker than D's or I's. These critters are the sweetest creatures around. All they want to do is help...and help. They want to sit in your lap, snuggle up with you and in general, just be with you. You make their day and they want to make yours! They want to help you anyway they can. S dogs are very stable in their personalities. They are generally not as excitable as D's or I's and usually bark a lot less. They avoid confrontation at all costs.

A dog that is a high S under stress can be very submissive. They will roll on their backs and display their abdomens to any situation that seems confrontational. These are generally your puppy pee'ers. With confrontation, they squat and urinate, then roll over and urinate ... they can be very submissive. In training an S puppy, it is very important to praise and praise and praise for the good things and emotionally ignore the accidents.

Anger, acrimony, loud words, even if not directed at the S dog, will see the S dog leave the room, hide under something and act like he or she was the cause of the problem. However, S types because they are so sweet and understanding hold the world together.

Early on, before knowledge of the D.I.S.C. system, I had a tendency to shout about Hannah's behavior. I might have said expressively: "Hannah, what are you doing!" and Joss would leave the room and go hide! Hannah would just look at me like: "What!?" S dogs and humans are always sorry for whatever happened to cause the emotional situation whether they are involved or not. Human S types will apologize for the weather, as if they could control it. Loud voices, harsh commands or emotional outbursts will just crush S types and make them unhappy. They carry around criticism with them for days. They love people and other dogs but will wait to be invited to play. They aren't pushy. They are really sweet dogs that want to help make your life better. S types seldom have any problems, unless they are treated harshly, then they just kind of disappear and act depressed. S dogs make great pets and good human companions. S's are nice.

The C behavioral style

These dogs and humans are the most reserved, the least social and may appear to be shy. They are very task oriented and statistically, the smartest part of the populations. In the D.I.S.C. model, we are at the lower left quadrant. C's are very analytical and love figuring things out. They love mysteries. Toys that make them work to get a treat are great for them. They are very quick to notice changes in detail. Acute changes in their life can create a lot of stress and behavioral issues. While they bark less than D's and I's, they will bark if they notice a new detail and want you to know that things have changed or are different than they normally are.

C's like a routine since they are very task oriented and love to work. Again, because they are reserved, these dogs hate confrontation, anger, acrimony, or loud emotional words. They are easy to make very submissive with anger and loud voices, so training has to be positive with praise and no negative reinforcements. It is easy to crush their personalities. Under negative circumstances, they may learn to tune you out and will never forget if you are unfair.

Our Joss was a C/S personality, so she was very detailed, non-confrontational and sweet. She loved to work (called play) and wouldn't quit unless she was totally exhausted. Even then, her eyes would move like she was watching us and ready to go but was obviously relieved when we would say "Enough, good girl!" In humans, the C type is the perfectionist. They notice only the trees, not the forest. The D, for example, only sees the forest, never the trees. Because of the way their brains work, the C styles make great watch dogs. They will keep the owners alert to what is going on both in and around the house. They aren't usually aggressive because they don't like confrontation unless their blend has D in it.

Lets look at a previous example in light of the D.I.S.C. system. Remember when we brought our dog Hannah home to Joss? Hannah was an I/D blend. Joss was a C/S. So we brought home a 6 month old I/D (we didn't know this system then) and she promptly began to harass and play with Joss. Hannah was truly a ssbbbb type of dog. She wanted to play, interact and have some fun!

So, she began to jump at Joss, pull at her hair and ears. You know, just party/party dog style! In a few days, we realized that Joss was acting rather strangely. She was very quiet, not eating so well, and very inactive. This was unusual, since Joss seldom ever stopped moving. Border Collies herd and our cats were fair game. As we watched, we realized that when Hannah would begin one of her I/D routines, Joss would nearly go catatonic! She would just stand there with her eyes looking at us, with her head down, seemingly depressed and glued to the floor.

Well, in hindsight, the wild I/D Hannah, loving activity and challenges, was giving Joss the works. Hannah was just doing her thing, nothing personal. All of us also do our own thing to others and it's nothing personal! However, Joss, the reserved C/S, was absolutely bewildered and wondered what we had brought into her home! She was truly in C/S hell. This was classic brain cross-wiring at its fullest. Joss disliked confrontation and Hannah was all confrontation and fun.

When Hannah got no response, she only took it up a notch and then Joss would get worse. My wife and I had to intervene by helping Joss assert herself and helping Hannah get herself under control. We did this by using techniques like giving Joss her food and treats first while making Hannah wait, by having Joss go out the door first with Hannah following and giving Hannah some new games so she would leave Joss alone whenever we could see the stress tickling the corners of Joss' eyes. We would insert the pack leader's wishes. As you recall, Joss and Hannah did become the best of friends. Our favorite photo is the one you have seen of Joss lying in a sunny spot on the carpet with Hannah sprawled over the top of her, both sound asleep.

With behavior problems, the secret for success is two fold. First, you must be consistent. Secondly, you must commit for the long term, definitely more than just a few days. Dogs, when well trained, are wonderful. When they are out of control, only out of control children are harder to live with. Many humans find the info we have been discussing hard to take. They feel that you should just bark out the orders, jerk the dog around so it will mind, but that's ineffective. Applying these easy observations will really make life a lot easier. Just like when we went to using a bell for Hannah's housetraining, going out for 'business' became fun and a challenge, two critical factors for an I/D style.

Let's review

D's are task oriented, outgoing and see the big picture (the forest). They are confrontational, love challenges and working. They make great companions and guard dogs whether they are a German shepherd guarding your home or a Chihuahua guarding your chair in front of the television. Training must be consistent and start early in life. Socialization is critical, since they are so task oriented. They are very bright dogs and easy to train. Training is just a task and a way to assert your pack leader status. Again, you praise the correct behavior, but don't confront them on the wrong behavior. If you confront them, they will challenge you and never forget if you flinch. Humans will nearly always flinch when it comes to dog challenges because we don't speak dog very well. D styles love to be pack leaders, even if the pack is all human. Good basic training creates a great life with a D style dog.

I's are people oriented and outgoing. They S.S.B.B.B.B. around life and their home. They are the most likely to bark and just go kind of nuts with excitement. They love to interact and are quick to follow you around the house to see what's up? "Are we going to party here or is it just a project?" They require very *fun* training but their attention span is short, so plan on being consistent, focusing on the long term. They are easily distracted. You don't want to wind up an I, they are already there! Their energy can wear you out! If you could bottle an I's energy and sell it, the world would be an active place.

S's are people oriented and more reserved. They just care. They want to be with you and do things with you. "Don't make me the center of attention but I'll love to help. And please, don't have any confrontations or angry words with or around me, I might melt!" Training needs to be with praise, not confrontations. They are the sweetest, most submissive, best companions, 'need you', 'love you,' type of dogs, and humans!

C's are task oriented and the most reserved. They see only the trees, not the forest, and every new thing around is interesting. Training needs to be with praise, not confrontation but make it interesting. Something new is always interesting to C's. They are working, detailed, most intelligent, analytical (love to figure things out), most shy, hate confrontation (actively avoids it), happy by themselves doing their own thing, perfect type of dogs ... and humans! You do not need to entertain them.

So, you now have a clue of how behavior in dogs and humans works. It is only a clue. Remember, these are only genetic 'hard-wired' behavioral strength tendencies that can be modified or trained. If you understand how these strengths apply, use praise for training and don't try to have an S-type do a D's job, life becomes a lot more stress free. This applies to dogs and to us. We are strongest when we are working in our strengths. We are happiest working in our genetic mold but can do anything we want, in any circumstance, instantly, if we realize what our tendencies are and know how to train our brain to get what we want. Brain plasticity, the ability to remodel or modify our brain function, enables us to create what we want in life, to add new skills and create new behaviors. It helps to know our natural strengths.

The key to all this info is that when you understand the other person or a dog's tendencies, it is easy to modify your style to enhance the relationship, communication and training. By applying this knowledge, we can make our world and the world around us a better place. Contact us if you would like to research your behavioral strengths. *You can reach us at:* www.bordercolliebrain.com

Dr. J'isms

1. Your genetic strengths can be defined.

2. Knowing your strengths creates effective training.

3. DISC is validated and proven.

4. Train your brain like you train a dog.

5. Trained strengths create success!

FUN PAGE
Your Doggie D.I.S.C.

1. Pick a pet in your life and apply the Doggie D.I.S.C. system.

2. Pick 2 people in your life and apply the Doggie D.I.S.C. system.

3. Write down how each in 1 and 2 differ or are the same in their behavior.

Pippin, Tucker, and Dr. J.
New relationships!

Chapter 12
Is This Your Puppy Or Is It You?

After decades of seeing literally thousands of puppies at the same ages, on the same exam tables, under the same settings, I can usually project to the new owners how their puppy will turn out. I can explain to the client that their puppy will take some consistent training and will be happiest when it is working or it may be a puppy that really needs to have some fun to respond to training and so forth. When the knowledge of the D.I.S.C. system was learned, I found out why I could be accurate with what I was telling my clients and helping them to increase their success with their pet at an earlier age, most of the time.

However, I continue to deal with the largest variable … the owners! Yes, I'm talking about you. If I want you to do certain things to make your life with your pet closer to perfect than to hell, I have to be able to communicate it in a way that locks it into your brain. Knowing your D.I.S.C. style tendencies is helpful. Cutting to the chase for a D client or listing all the details for a high C keeps the client happy, decreases my stress and the puppies or kittens get a jump start on a trained life and relationships that will last.

People will train their four-legged children but don't do so well with their two-legged ones. The species here are different but the principles are the same. For example, we had to hide our trash containers in the exam rooms just to keep the kids out of them. Amazingly, we will train our pets and leave our children and our own brains out of the training loop. Our untrained pets may make our life miserable but our untrained children will eventually be running the world! Pets, children and we all respond to 'Border Collie brain training!'

Speaking of you, remember that dogs feel you are just funny looking dogs that don't speak dog very well. They observe our behavior (*Chap. 13, the Russians*) and draw dog behavior conclusions from it and we aren't even aware that they are assessing us. If we would adopt some of their behavioral traits, the world would be a better place. At least, our part of it would be.

Take some time and just observe your pets. If you don't have a pet, borrow one from a friend or go to a park where pets are on display. Just sit and watch them eat, walk, sniff, and sleep. When students think they want to be a veterinarian or a veterinary technician, I recommend that they spend time just watching dogs, or cats, or horses, or cows, or hogs, whatever species they are interested in. Knowing what is normal is the basis for knowing what is abnormal. This applies to you and all the lives you touch, including a pet. You can be taught what is abnormal but you must first learn what is normal.

In diagnostic medicine, some things that appear abnormal are actually normal. The education that veterinarians receive is focused on diagnosing what is abnormal and treating it. Nearly everything you see during a veterinary medical education is a referral from another veterinarian. They are, generally, unusual or complicated cases. To a newly graduated veterinarian *normal* animals can be boring. They want to feel the excitement of what they saw in college. They want dramatic cases, dramatic surgeries and other disasters. But as one's career progresses, the abnormal becomes routine and the normal should become a joy.

Here are two quick personal examples from early in my career. The first was right out of school. I had another veterinarian's client (*he was out of town*) show up for a c-section on her Boston Terrier. This was her prized female, a national champion. I had never performed a c-section before but knew the procedure and had assisted when at university. The spinal block and mild sedative worked well and I had quickly delivered one very weird looking puppy. The Boston terrier face was all deformed, the rear legs went straight back and seemingly had no joints. It was a breathing gelatinous looking blob but I sent it out to the owner while I closed the abdomen and finished the surgery. If it survived, I was certain I would be putting that puppy to sleep. The owner's instructions were firm: Whatever I delivered, she wanted it immediately. I could hear shouting in the exam room and wondered if the deformed gelatinous looking mess had already died.

I quickly learned that these were shouts of excitement and joy. The owner felt the markings on this puppy were the best she had ever seen and she had seen a lot of Boston puppies. To her, he was stunningly beautiful. What I thought was a gelatinous looking deformed thing turned out to be her greatest Champion Boston Terrier of all time. He was the one in a lifetime dog that breeders dream about. The owner knew what was normal, I certainly didn't.

The second one wasn't quite so dramatic, but I was really fortunate. I didn't put this puppy through any misery while I could learn what was normal in this case. The first German Shepherd puppy I saw in practice came in with perfectly erect, perky ears. What a puppy. He was intelligent, good natured and curious: a perfect dog.

Two weeks later, the client called and said her puppy had broken an ear and it would ruin him for being a show dog. They came in immediately and sure enough, one ear was broken. The left ear was perfect, standing to attention. The right ear was lying nearly flat on the side of his head. When I picked it up, it promptly flopped back down. One ear looked like a German shepherd, the other a coonhound. The owner was right. The 'coonhound' ear appeared broken.

On exam, however, the cartilage seemed smooth and straight but the ear just wouldn't stay up. I hated to splint the ear because splinting has a tendency to make puppies head shy with all that *stuff* banging around their head. If bandaged when they are puppies, as adults, they are a little spooky about motion around their head. So, after discussion, the owners agreed with me that we ought to see if it would get well on its own over time. Sure enough, in about 10 days, they called to say the ear was normal again! It must have just been sprained! Well, hooray for that! We all celebrated until they called about a week later saying that the ear was really bad this time. His show dog career might be over before it started.

They came zipping in and sure enough, the ear was down. They knew of nothing that might have caused it. I checked my notes and found that I had written down that it was the other ear the first time. Once we all got our heads together and discussed the issue, we all agreed. The second 'down' ear was the 'other' one and the owners felt it must be somehow contagious from ear to ear. We had to treat it. We didn't. That *sprained* ear healed much like the first one. His show career wasn't illustrious but his ears were perfect. Taking a good, detailed medical history can be critical!

Shortly after these episodes, I realized that a very fast growing large breed puppy that had erect ears was prone to have the ears go up and down during acute growth spurts. The key was that if the ears were ever normal as a puppy, they would eventually become normal as an adult. However, if the ears were never up, they never would be. Genetics usually wins out when it comes to ears.

Our own genetics usually win out in our lives, but it doesn't have to. We can train ourselves to get what we want out of life in spite of our genetics or we can identify our genetics and use our strengths to be successful. However, as all careers go, the abnormal becomes routine and the normal becomes a joy. I have great memories of my patients and their people.

When I didn't have a clue about a case, I knew it was unusual. I have learned that when this occurs, every veterinarian or physician should quickly seek a second opinion from a specialist. Specialists are on the cutting edge of knowledge and technology. They see the strange and the weird cases. They have an experienced database in their specialty that no practitioner can match or find on line. Ego shouldn't dictate the quality of medicine. Ego shouldn't dictate whether an animal lives or dies. The choices are and should always be yours, as the client, for the health of you and your pet.

If your medical professionals aren't listening to you and the health issues for you or your pet aren't being resolved, what choice should you make? Your medical professionals, veterinary or medical, are part of your team but you are the team leader. You must be the advocate for you and your pet. It may not be easy to stand up for what you want but if you won't, who will? So, again, is it your puppy or kitten we are talking about here or is it you? You make the call!

Dr. J'isms

1. Humans have an impact on everything.

2. Children are just little humans.

3. First, know what is normal

4. First, prevent. Last, treat.

4. If we don't care, no one will.

FUN PAGE
Are You A Puppy?

1. List 3 things that you used to think were weird or abnormal but you are ok with today. Ex. Democrats, Republicans or Tea Party.

2. Write under each one why your attitudes have changed. Ex. New info.

3. Training entails taking good patterns and applying them in new situations. See how you can apply these patterns to other situations in your life. Just knowing these good patterns are there in your life will cause you to use them for your success.

Ozzie, a Russian Grizzly Bear, mostly a vegetarian, just observing

Chapter 13
You And The Russians

In Chapter 12, we saw that our pets learn through observation. Sitting back and observing what goes on around us, including our own behavior is a healthy strategy. Looking at our life as if it's a movie and we are in the audience is a great activity.

I can tell you a true human observation and conclusion story that happened to me. In the late 1990's through a U.S. Congressional-Rotary-Methodist program, young Russians that were business leaders in their careers came to the U.S. and toured for 10 days around Topeka to learn about our society, culture, business and legal structure. I was one of the point people to organize this ten day tour representing Rotary. In setting up the tour, we had them meet with the Mayor, the Governor, local businessmen and women, religious leaders and Rotary clubs in northeast Kansas. It was a lot of work and really out of my comfort zone. I grew up herding cattle, hogs and sheep, but people? It is rather like herding cats. However, I volunteered to help, so it was self-inflicted trauma. Yes, I have a lot of the D.I.S.C. style S in me and so do most veterinarians and their teams!

The first few days I drove the twelve passengers van and took them to where we were to meet people and tour their businesses. While the Russians had some English skills, a few did not and only 2 had been to the U.S. before. I found them to be a courteous group but very reserved and quiet. They smiled occasionally and appeared interested but there was obviously some culture shock. En route, they had stopped in New York and Washington, D.C. for a few days before coming to Topeka, so I knew it shouldn't be jet lag and was a little concerned that we weren't showing them what they wanted to see.

After the first 3 days, I received a phone call from one of the more outgoing Russians who spoke English fairly well. The call came late at night after I had gone to sleep. The Russian team had just returned from some socializing with their host families at local watering holes and he had a question. He said to me: "Doug, you seem like a nice guy. If I asked you a question, would you tell me the truth?" I shook the cobwebs out of my head and replied, "Sure!" He then asked me if I was C.I.A.! I almost answered jokingly: "No, I'm F.B.I.!" Fortunately, I didn't. He was serious, very serious. The Russians wanted to know.

The question was a result of their cultural background. The Russians felt that the whole tour was a set-up just for them. What they were seeing didn't really represent what America was all about. I had been their tour guide those first few days and they had been watching. He explained that they felt that I must be "the big guy!" When I asked what that meant, he went on to explain that in their culture at that time, titles or position meant nothing. If they went to a party or a meeting, they had been taught to watch for and observe the one person that everyone knew. They watched for the one in the room that everyone greeted first. The one that was walked up to first was the *big guy or gal*.

When touring around N.E. Kansas, I was always the first one to be greeted at each new stop and the people in charge usually came to me first to shake hands. It was repeated over and over again. Whether it was the mayor, the governor or business leaders it always went like this, "Hey, Doug or Dr. Jernigan, or Dr. J! Welcome, come on in, have a doughnut and coffee. Introduce us to the team."

You understand that I was the tour guide and knew everyone the team was visiting. I was being greeted as is normal in our custom. The Russians didn't know that. Of course, I could assure him and the team, that I was not C.I.A. I explained that the tour and what they were seeing was a typical Kansas American experience, not a C.I.A. front that was just for their benefit. The next morning, I took them on a tour of my veterinary practice to meet my practice partner and team to confirm what we had discussed. They had believed, based on their own experiences and what they had been taught as children, that this was all only for their benefit! We were just running a capitalistic scam.

The impact on their behavior was immediate. It was as if the sunshine had come on in their lives. What an outstandingly intelligent, fun loving and enthusiastic group they had become overnight and continued to be for the rest of our time together. We had a ball for the rest of the tour with all of our guides and experiences.

The point of this story is that our pets watch to see who the pack leader is. It is a normal strategy for our pets. You could say that the Russians were applying our pet's strategy. Observation is a lot more than watching or looking. Observation is about seeing! This 'observation strategy' can be a factor leading to success and we should begin practicing it in our own lives!

Because of that genetic tendency in the reptilian part of our brain, that Border Collie part, humans can benefit from using dog traits. These young Russians were doing exactly what a dog would do by observing and reacting to what they saw.

Now let's talk control and communication. The way to control things in our lives is to respond to events as our pets do. The only control we have in life is how we respond to what happens to us and around us. Remember this because I'll refer to this again a little later. Communication, on the other hand, is about everything except language. Your pets communicate with you all the time and can't speak a word of human. You communicate with your pets all the time and can't speak a word of dog, cat, cow, hog or horse. Spend some time acting like a dog or a young Russian leader and learn something. Observe what is going on around you and decide if you want to respond to it!! You don't have to, it's a choice. Don't let what is happening around you dictate how you will behave or feel. Doing this will enhance your career, your health, your relationships and your future!

The Russians expressed that they felt the most outstanding American trait is that we have such energy and drive. If we want to get something done, Americans just do it. We also have a legal system that didn't exist in Russia at that time. The cultural environment here is business oriented. We set up non-profit organizations to advocate for programs or people. We have a freedom of speech that gets well used (and abused?) that just wouldn't fly in Russia in the late 1990's. There is nothing more fun than spending time with intelligent, enthusiastic and interactive people. It's exceeded only by being around well-trained pets and children!!

Dr. J'isms

1. Our pets don't just watch, they see!

2. Communication is not just words.

3. Seeing creates knowledge.

4. Action based on knowledge creates success!

FUN PAGE
You And Who?

1. Make a list of 20 items in the area around you that you can see.

2. For each item, list how long it has been since you really looked at it and noticed it.

3. Now, go look in your bathroom and see how clean it really is through your **new** observing eyes!

Hannah demonstrating the promised land of poop and pee on command!

Chapter 14
Housetraining And Habits

So, Russians are great people, but let's go back to dogs. The nice thing about dogs is that their genetic schedule works well around our typical workday. Wolves and coyotes get up early, hunt for a few hours, and then spend the day snoozing or sleeping and other wolf or coyote stuff but not doing much. Late in the afternoon or early evening, they hunt again, socialize until midnight or so, and then they will sleep. So, if you are worried about your dog during the day, he or she isn't worried about you! With a new puppy, I always start my clients off with the housetraining talk. This is directly related to a successful relationship that lasts.

1. Feed them on a schedule

I recommend twice a day. Free feeding complicates effective housetraining. If fed on a schedule, a dog poops on a schedule. This makes it easier for us to get them outside for their 'business' and to make sure they are 'running on empty' when they come back in the house. I recommend that clients use a one syllable word or short phrase to associate with taking them out to have their stools or urinating. If you train up a dog in the way it should go, it will. Pick any word you like, but use only that word or short phrase consistently. The rest of your pack, the two-legged ones, should also use the same word so your pet doesn't get confused.

2. Praise with consistency is important for pet or human

Praise your puppy and yourself when you get the results you want. If a puppy 'goofs' inside the house do not react in any way, physically, emotionally or verbally. The behavior that gets the largest emotional response from you will become the behavior of choice for a puppy and you.

The same principle applies to humans. When we say, "Oh, heck, I always do that!" or "Oh, here I go again!", we are creating emotional moments that tell our brain to log it into the hard drive (Border Collie) part of our brain and repeat the behavior when needed! When was the last time you said to yourself: "Way to go! It's ann outstanding job. You're smarter every day. You did really well! Let's do that again! I'm so smart!"

What? Do you think that doing this sounds stupid? It doesn't sound any more stupid than the negatives we repeat so quickly to ourselves. Whether we are talking to our dog or ourselves, someone (your Border Collie brain?) is listening and storing that information for future action! The principle of praise is important. I had clients housetrain their dog to poop and pee inside their home by getting angry or yelling: "No, no, no!!" then chasing it around the house after they had an accident. My clients quickly created the greatest game a puppy can learn. It's called the, "I can get you to chase me, chase me and chase me whenever I want by the poop and pee game." All puppies learn how to start that game! They can also quickly learn the correct game, as long as we play it with consistent praise for good behavior and emotionally ignoring the incorrect behavior. We choose at which game they learn to excel!

We do the same thing in our own lives. We have learned the praise the negative game in most of our lives and are pretty good at it. Whatever behavior gets the greatest emotional response is what our brain records and attempts to reproduce in the future. Our training began early in life by our sincere, well-meaning parents, teachers and playmates when we were children. Our bosses, supervisors, spouses and friends may have continued the game and we play it with ourselves when we are alone. Most of us are very good at this game. We may have passed it on to our own children. It hinders all of us.

However, with equal speed, we can learn to praise the correct behaviors and learn not to emotionally reward the wrong behaviors. It works, it works and it works. The concept is easy, application is simple and the results are wonderful. If we can housetrain our pets to the use the promised land of poop and pee, we can train ourselves to obtain whatever we want in life.

Now, let's go back to your puppies, your home and the pooping ground. Puppies think of doing their business only 4 times during their life. No, not 4 times total, in 4 situations that occur all the time! When you and your family lock these next 4 keys into your mind, housetraining a dog is easy.

Key #1: When a puppy first wakes up.

This includes:
A. The first noise in the morning. Whoever causes the first noise, gets to take the puppy out. It includes rain, snow or wind.
B. After any nap, even if it is just 10-15 minutes long. When that puppy wakes up, stretches and looks around, he or she is thinking about taking care of business and needs to go out. Again, give a lot of praise for doing it right in the right place at the right time. For some puppies, a small piece of stool in the area you want them to go will help stimulate both types of puppy business.

Key #2: Right after eating.

The gastro-colic (stomach-colon) reflex in puppies is pretty active. Food in the stomach causes the G.I. tract to begin moving, including the colon. It's like when a train engine starts up, it takes a minute, but the caboose will move! As I said, feeding twice daily is plenty for most puppies. Letting a puppy eat as much as it wants twice daily is the right amount. Some of the tiny breeds, due to liver issues need special diets and different schedules, so I recommend you talk to your veterinarian with those breeds.

I recommend that you follow the guidelines on the bag, but realize that dog food companies like to sell dog food, so the amounts recommended to eat are usually high for our sedentary pets. If a puppy is really hungry after the food is gone, it needs more! If they aren't eating all of it, pick it up after they walk away from it. Leaving it down for 15-20 minutes is usually long enough for them to fill their stomach.

This applies only to puppies. Adult dogs, like adult humans, need to have their diet quantity and quality controlled. We want only lean, happy, energetic dogs, not something that looks and moves like the average North American! Generally, if you feed twice daily with a high quality diet, you get two solid 'business' samples daily in the pooping ground. When they poop, they usually will pee after a few minutes or vice versa.

When you realize that food is the only thing you are putting into your pet (or your body) consistently, I recommend you spend a little money for it. The difference between the really cheap diets and the premium diets is pennies a day. Studies (human and animal) have shown that the highest quality diets add years of healthy life.

On the practical side, really cheap diets produce a lot more volume of softer, sometimes runny, stools that are hard to predict, for both you and your puppy. These mushy stools are a lot harder to clean up in the yard and a lot messier on your shoes.

Key #3

Right after chewing on a toy, a rawhide or your favorite pair of shoes. Wait, wait ... no emotional outbursts! Chewing does the same thing as eatin. Duh! When they get up, stretch and look around after chewing on a toy, they are thinking of business principles.

Key #4: Right after playing.

What we are talking about here is being a cracker dog in the house, roaring around, running, barking, chasing air squirrels, in other words, just being exercise silly. We have all watched our dogs go ripping around the house for no good reason (when was the last time you felt like doing that?) and having a great time. When they slow down and stop, they are thinking about you know what! Anytime a puppy starts to look around, they are thinking of anointing something with something, somewhere and soon! It's time to get them outside! Give lots of praise, well, for lots!

These are the big 4 of house training. They aren't 100% effective but they'll take most puppies to the promised land of poop and pee on command. This really comes in handy when you are traveling or in a hurry to leave the house! Dogs, like us, require three weeks or more for their brains to lay down the neurological highway of a new habit.

They will appear housetrained before those three weeks are up. Continue to be consistent and never emotionally react if they goof up in the house. Here it is again: Remember, negative behavior should get no emotional reaction. Positive behavior should get a lot of positive attention (hooray! Rah, rah, rah, sis, boom, bah!!), including small bits of treat if a puppy is very food oriented. Trust me, it's ok to get excited about poop and pee in your puppies early years! It was a large part of my career!

So, why focus on this? Well, it's good advice for you and your pet. It works because whatever gets the most attention, the greatest emotional response, creates the most endorphins in the system. These endorphins pop open the hard drive of your and your pet's brains. This particular event then gets recorded in the hard drive of their and our Border Collie brains. Once recorded, these events are the quickest to be recalled. Do we want our pets to remember the thrill of going business or the thrill of being chased around the house game! Do we want to have the thrill of victory in our lives or the agony of defeat? We choose by what we praise ... for our pets and ourselves!

The **housetraining praise principle** applies to humans and our human relationships. We usually forget the praise side but are quick on the emotionally reactive, negatively correcting side. Where do you think gossip comes from? Why do you think we trash others to make ourselves feel better?

Stop it now! It's a choice based on training. Praise your children, spouse, friends, co-workers or employees for what is going right but forget the chase me, chase me, hit me with a newspaper, rub my nose in it response and your world will be a lot more fun! People around you will think you are a lot more intelligent than you probably are.

My clients always gave me skeptical looks when I talk about these housetraining principles but I asked them to try it for 10 days to 2 weeks and then check in with me to see how it's going. Some puppies are easier than others but the never made it to the promised land of poop and pee puppies are usually our own fault. Not always but usually. Our own, "I can't do that, I'll never succeed, it will always be like this," lives are the same. Some brains, pet and human, are just defective and nothing works well but that is extremely rare. It's unlikely that your brain is defective. You just haven't trained it yet.

One truly defective brain trait commonly seen in practice is found in Persian cats. I know, don't send me the letters but if I had a client's cat that was having litter box usage problems of any type, it probably will be a Persian or a Persian mix. It is so consistent, that if a client calls in about a litter box usage problem, when I get on the phone, my first comment will be, "How old of a Persian is your kitty?" While it's not a high percentage of Persian cats that have this problem, if it's your Persian, it's 100%!

Even though this is a cat example, it is an example of a defective brain. Their land of poop and pee is anywhere and everywhere their eye can see whenever the urge hits. Many of these cats just can't figure out that a litter box has a consistent purpose. You can't train these cats to a litter box. They might hit it occasionally, but it's only by accident. The corollary in humans is the male human that never puts the lid down! This human brain defect is much more common than the Persian cat one but it can usually be trained out of existence. Women can only hope.

If a human has ever housetrained and then successfully taught obedience commands to a dog, they can make wonderful parents. When we realize that children are really just two-legged dogs, we become effective parents. However, it is common to see a well-behaved, obedient dog and children that make ants look calm in the same exam room. In order to get the, "I love and respect you" look you see in your pet's eyes reflected in your children's eyes, use the same principles we have just discussed. It works, no matter what the species.

When it comes to your life, remember that dogs think you are just funny looking dogs that don't speak dog very well. They observe our behavior and draw dog behavior conclusions from it. They are actively learning about us and we don't even know realize it. The techniques and principles that we use to housetrain our pets are excellent for using to train ourselves for the future we want. These same principles also apply to our children. We can only control how we respond to what happens around us. We can create a life that is full of fun and less filled with stress if we will just apply these principles. So, treat yourself and others like a dog!

Dr. J'isms

1. Praise creates the best habits.

2. It takes 3 consistent weeks of praise for a new habit.

3. Puppies are house trained by the above keys.

4. What we eat determines our energy.

5. What we praise, we believe.

6. What we believe, we act on.

7. What we act on becomes our future!

FUN PAGE
Your Housetraining Habits

1. Spend 3 days noticing your comments about yourself and others. Write down the good and 'not so good'.

2. On your list, draw a line through all the negative items and stop using them.

3. On your list, draw a circle around the good items and start using them a lot. Add to your good list everything good you can think up and start using them a lot.

Is Pippin really just a dog on drugs?

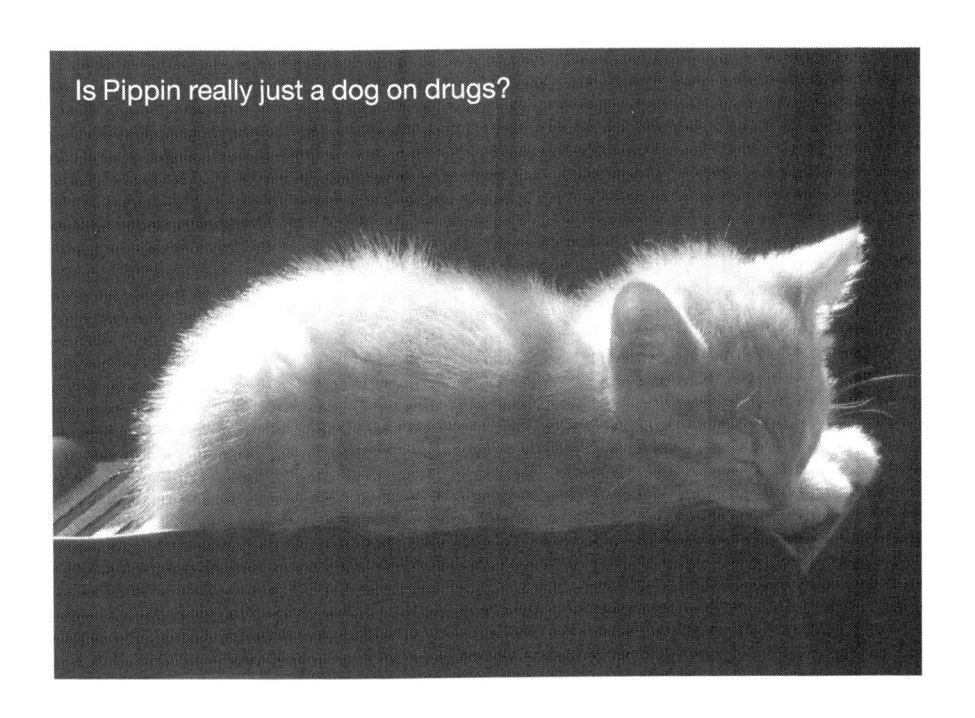

Chapter 15
Training Them, Training Us

Train your brain and don't live by default! If you get the idea that accomplishing goals is similar to training a dog, you are correct. First of all, you can't get a dog's attention by just thinking about it. You have to take some action. You have to speak to it. For us, it is scientifically well documented that self-talk is one of the quickest ways to create change in our lives.

When you first speak to your brain, it feels funny. You will feel like you are faking it. You are! It feels like you are talking to yourself. You are talking to yourself! However, if you realize that your genetic *Border Collie* part of your brain is like a program running in the background of your cranial computer, you'll begin to get it. When you realize that this part of our brain is continually modifying what you are trying to do, you'll realize that you do have to train your brain! It either runs us or we run it. If it runs us, we are living by default. We either have an obedient dog or we have a wild dog between the ears. When we self-talk, we are training our brain to be obedient. Here is how and when this occurs.

We already self-talk all the time and have been since we started to be verbal. When we talk, our brain has to listen. What we say changes what we believe. What we believe changes what we do. What we do changes our present and our future! Therefore, we need to be careful about what we say to ourselves. Training our brains is EXACTLY like training a dog. It helps if you go with the D.I.S.C. strengths and as all dogs need obedience training, so does your brain! Some training is better than no training. Why do you think we go to school as children? It could more accurately be called going to brain training!

As with a dog, we should use simple commands that have emotional connections. Using repetition with consistency is critical. The good news is that you, not someone else, is training your brain! It's not the television, the radio, the drugs, your preacher, your rabbi, your neighbor, or your brother-in-law, Harry! It's you. You are the trainer of your brain. You are not your brain. Your brain is just a Border Collie that needs training. Are you beginning to get the drift here? That bright eyed, tail wagging, perky eared, raring to go Border Collie is between your ears! you are in charge either on purpose or by default.

In summary, self-talk will start you on your path to success. Just like training a dog, self-talk about what you want (Come, sit, down!), not what you have or are afraid of. Whatever you say to yourself will become your reality! We read in the last chapter that you should praise yourself for the good and eliminate the negative talk. Like a dog, you can train yourself into the good or into the negative. You can learn to poop and pee in the house or in the yard. You choose. What you have in your life right now, at some level, you have chosen. If you like what you have: Congratulations! If you don't like what you have, **choose differently**! There are good references out there about the science of self-talk where you can get as much or as little detail as you want, but I have just summarized hours of seminars into a training manual for your brain, courtesy of your pet!

With self-talk, you must take some action to get what you want. All the clichés apply. You know, "A ship without a rudder, a single step starts a journey of a thousand miles, if you don't know where you are going, you'll get there, if you think you can or you can, you are right!" Great quotes behind great ideas but in dog words, "Ready? Fetch! Go, go, go and go!! Good dog!"

Dr. J'isms

1. Training our brain requires self-talk
2. Self-talk means talking to your self.
3. Talking to your self seems strange.
4. Your brain listens to you best.
5. Consistent emotional praise creates success.

In continuing our housetraining and habits topic, let's talk about humans, dogs and cats! When clients were in the exam and obviously expecting a child or have just added a new pack member, if I knew them well, I would always give them a human training edge, a nugget of training gold that'll make their family life better. I will tell them, "New humans have to be taught to come, sit, heel, down and stay by the age of 3!" It always gets a smile but I would tell them that I'm serious! If you don't have a child's attention by the age of 3, life only gets tougher for you and your children! I've watched it evolve over and over for 35+ years in my office!

I have four wonderful children, now self-supporting well-adjusted adults and two grandsons. My two youngest are twin sons. Yes, when they were born, I had to endure all the, "Do all veterinarians have litters?" I tell clients that even in adulthood, if I say, "Boys, sit!" They would look around for a chair! I'm proud of all my children. They didn't always have me around to help. Training works! Ok, that sounds kind of harsh, but puppies or children do not need to be spanked, pounded, chased, whacked or threatened. They need to be praised for the correct behavior and have the negative behavior emotionally ignored. Praise, praise, praise and praise are really important. The earlier in their development you start this, the earlier the success. However, in humans, if you decide to say, "NO!" It's the same in dogs. Make sure it is "NO!" today, tomorrow and forever. It's called consistency! Being consistent in training creates security for the recipient. Children and animals want to know where the, "line that shouldn't be crossed" exists. Even if they want to cross it in the beginning.

Recall that Joss was trained to know that the upstairs area of our home was the cat haven. She wasn't allowed. She spent all of her life, after being trained, waiting at the bottom of the stairs if the cats were upstairs. We thought we heard her coming down the stairs one evening, but by the time we got to the bottom of the stairs, her eyes said: "It wasn't me!"

During parts of the day or evening, her head would be on the bottom step, her eyes would be pointed upward, watching and waiting for cats, but she wouldn't go up to the haven. Okay, maybe that once! So, if you train a dog well, they won't break the rules whether or not you are there. If you train your brain well, it won't break the rules either.

Cats, if trained, won't break the rules if you are present. As soon as you are out of sight they will do what they want. For cats, I believe that our sight is truly out of mind! Cats can be as easily trained as dogs, it just requires a little different strategy. It takes persistence. Cats spend 60-80% of their lives sleeping. They sleep because they have a lot of serotonin in their brains. They live a life that is just a little hazy unless a mouse is in the room.

So really, cats are just dogs on drugs!' When you say something to a dog, they react! All terriers react in a nanosecond. However, terriers may have forgotten why they were reacting by the time they look at you! To train cats, you have to realize that many things are in *slow motion* to them, so they react in a delayed style. As I said, persistence is required in a cat, as in a dog, but with a capital P for cats! I have had clients and one of my brothers train cats to come, sit, shake, and play fetch. So if you are working at training a cat, don't give up and remember the haziness! Oh, if you can train a cat well, you can do anything you want with your life.

Okay, cats live in a little bit of a haze, but you gotta' love 'em, just like some of the hazy people in your life! We used to play a game with our first Abby, Khamsin. It was throw the playing card into the air and let Khami kill it! He loved this game! These flat birds would fly across the room. Khami would leap up and knock them out of the air, then "kill" it by pouncing on it. If the 'bird' should land on its edge up against a wall or a piece of furniture, he wasn't satisfied. It wasn't dead yet. He'd keep on pounding it until it was flat and completely dead. He never tired of that game and neither did we. Khami had his own set of playing cards. They were the ones with the holes in them! What can we learn from Khami's game? If we can find a game like that to keep us going non-stop toward our goals, our lives will change!

Dr. J'isms

1. Early *brain* training makes life fun!

2. Consistent training creates success!

3. Praise the good!

4. Emotionally ignore the negative!

5. Cats are, "dogs on drugs"!

6. Make your life a game!

FUN PAGE
Training You, You And You

1. Spend 5 minutes writing down how your life is fun. Set the clock and go. Ex. I really enjoy it when a new puppy comes into the office.

2. Read what you have written out loud, for your ears only.

3. Spend 5 minutes writing and then read out loud what you would like your life to be.

An early winter day before the lake freezes.
Lake Simcoe, Innisfil, Ontario, Canada.

Chapter 16
Gooooals!

Hooray!! Goal planning. Most people say grooooooan. However, if you aren't happy doing what you are doing, enjoying what you have and don't know where you are headed, some goal planning may be needed. If you aren't all fired up about something, how will you get what you want? Simple? Yes! Easy? Yes! What? Two yeses? Yes!

Many of you have seen many strategies about goal planning, but no one has told you that you are really just a Border Collie that needs some training! Pointers already know how to hunt. Border Collies already know how to herd.

Dachshunds already know how to be bullheaded. All of these breeds need training to use what they already know effectively in new venues.

Like them, you already know how to goal plan effectively! You are a goal-planning machine! Trust me, you already know how to goal plan successfully and with enthusiasm. You are successful daily! You just need to apply your skills in a new way.

Most adults and most children goal plan and accomplish their goals all the time, every day, multiple times a day. They are really good at it and so are you! If you have well trained a dog, it makes no difference if you are putting it through its paces in your home, in *Madison Square Garden* or in the open country! Everything your Border Collie knows in one place is the same applied somewhere else! The environment changes but the skills do not. Humans, though, seem to think that we have situational training, but your brain does not. The Border Collie in your head herds, no matter where it is! Here comes the example, a human one, not a doggie one.

Let's go on vacation! You want to go and have decided to go on vacation. This shows us what you want and a commitment to it. The next thing you do, usually, is to decide when you want to go. It wouldn't be smart if you wanted to go to the beach to pick Innisfil, Ontario (a city and province of Canada, eh?) in the month of January! See photo above! Beaches are wonderful on Lake Simcoe in July, but not in January! So, make what you want realistic. Now you have **want-commitment-when**. Most of us would write this down so we wouldn't forget what we wanted, what we were committed to and when we want to do it! It's effective to start making a list of items to look forward to!

Then, the little questions, "How do we get there, when do we have to leave, when are we coming back, how do we pay for it, what clothes should we to take, which children to take, should we take any children, should we take the dogs, should our spouse go, is it for relaxation or activities like beach, sleeping golfing tour..." and the list goes on and on and on! It is about this point that we begin to think that the pain of going on a vacation is greater than the fun, right? No, No, not about going on our holiday! We zip through that list of painful details like a Jack Russell terrier through a Kleenex! It's gone in a blizzard of head shaking! What just happened? Where did that blizzard of Kleenex come from? Is it because we like all the detail? No, it's because we are focusing on the pleasure, the fun and the goal!

It's the fourteen-year-old arthritic dog that is barely able to move around the house. If this joint creaking, muscle wasted old dog should spy a rabbit, it becomes a thundering engine of hair and slobber roaring across the yard and sending the rabbit zigzag sprinting away.

When the prize (goal) is "want" enough, the facts don't count. Yep, when the *want* is big enough, the facts don't count. This 14 year old dog is thinking… "YES! Close, so close, I'm so fired up!" and the rabbit is thinking, "Wow, that old dog can move, who would have imagined that?"

So, how big is your rabbit and how quick are you! It's a Kleenex, not a mountain! If you **Jack Russell Terrier want it**, you cannot fail! The old dog didn't catch the rabbit primarily because the rabbit was zigzag sprinting. Your personal goals are set in concrete. If you take the 'old dog thundering engine of hair and slobber' approach, you will meet your goals. It's a done deal! Yes, you must take some action, but if you want that rabbit badly enough, action is automatic. It will happen! If a want is big enough it will cause action.

Now, let's talk about the list of details that you just ripped through a minute ago. All life and business goals have details but now you know that you can rip through them at home, Madison Square Garden or out in the country! The environment doesn't count. Review it. We have want/commitment/when/fiddly details/thundering engine of hair and slobber = success!! Easy, eh?

In summary, write it down, read it out loud, for your ears only. Do the W.C.W.F.T.=S approach and you are on your way. Effective goal planning involves concrete and sand!!

CONCRETE!! **Goals need to be set in concrete.** You need to do all the above things to make it happen and then pour the concrete! It needs to be a realistic want (W), have commitment (C), put a date on it (W), rip through the fiddly details (F) and have a thundering engine (T) effort to create success (S). Next, we need to really focus as in dog chases rabbit focus and go for it. We want no distractions, no life happens stuff, no nothing…only action!! So, the goal is in concrete, immovable, easy to see, emotionally attractive and creates satisfyingly, excited all fired up, run, rabbit, run enthusiasm!!

SAND! **Your plans need to be set in sand.** The goal is to catch the rabbit. It's set in concrete. It doesn't change. Your plans are dependent on what happens when you thunder out of the door and start after the rabbit! Catching the rabbit can be an elusive proposition. A real rabbit will run, dart, jump and zigzag to make capture difficult. Adjusting to the run, dart, jump and zigzag of accomplishing our goals is our sandy plans.

We must have sandy plans. They may vary from day to day, hour to hour or even minute to minute. Rabbits scuttle about. Our focus must be on the goal. This requires go get-em, look 'em in the eye, body moving and head swiveling focus in action! Like chasing the rabbit, our plans must vary depending on what is working and what isn't. Sandy plans shift depending on what is and what isn't taking us closer to our set in concrete goal.

In contrast, many of us put our plans in concrete. "I'm headed for that corner of the yard today. I hope the rabbit is there." It's an attitude that only causes frustration and a sense of failure. We must have sandy plans to reach a concrete goal. When we have concrete plans, we create sandy goals. Sound familiar? Sandy goals don't make for a happy life! Sandy goals are hard to accomplish. Sandy goals make us think we can't accomplish goals. Deciding to run in a straight line toward the rabbit and never swerving wouldn't make for very many rabbit stew meals, would it?

The good news is that we get to choose. We have concrete goals with sandy plans or concrete plans with sandy goals. Failure is caused by sandy goals and concrete plans. Success is created by concrete goals and sandy plans!

Watch what is happening in pursuing your goals, listen to conditions, but keep everything moving forward. It isn't good enough to bark at the rabbit, we must pursue it like that thundering engine of hair and slobber if we want rabbit stew. Like a rabbit chase, the quicker we act, the harder we run, the more focused we are with no distractions or life happens events, the more rabbits we will have!

Dr. Doug Jernigan

Dr. J'isms

1. We reach goals daily
2. Our want must be big.
3. Goals in concrete.
4. Plans in sand.
5. Be a "thundering engine of hair and slobber" success!

FUN PAGE

Yoooour Gooooooals!

1. Write down the W.C.W.F.T.=S of your last vacation or holiday.

2. Write down the W.C.W.F.T.=S of your last work project.

3. Write down the W.C.W.F.T.=S of your major life goal and do it!

Are we leading "rabbit" lives?

Chapter 17
The Rabbit Interlude

I love rabbits. They are such cute creatures. Little twitchy noses, ears like radar for sound and their eyes see everything that moves. But, an unsuccessful rabbit is lunch. Did you know that rabbit stools are considered hors d'oeuvres for dogs? The protein and B vitamins in a rabbit's stool are delicacies to a dog. After all these years of practice, I'm convinced that rabbit stools are the truffles of the kingdom of dogs.

Hannah, a typical dachshund who is all nose and energy, would spend her sunny afternoons in our yard searching out these *bunny bonbons* and gobbling them down like M&Ms if she had the opportunity. It's one of the reasons that Hannah, like your cell phone, has limited 'free roaming' time in our fenced yard. While I have never tasted one (rabbit stools, not M&Ms), it is one of the reasons my dogs have not, do not, will not ever, drink from my water glass or lick my plate clean or kiss me on my lips. Think about where that tongue has been!! Some things Mother taught us just make a lot of sense! Sorry, just a bit of regression into practical pet ownership and human public health.

Rabbits, really, are just meals on wheels. Ask any dog and you'll find a different perspective than that of your four year old daughter! A rabbit's life is spent trying not to be a meal. Kits, baby rabbits, as they grow try not to be appetizers or dessert. I personally think that all rabbits should eat only weeds. If they did, they would live to a great old age. I'm also glad that I'm not a rabbit.

Does anything occur to you about now? Can you see where this is headed? How about application for our lives? How are you spending your life? Do you spend it "not being a meal" for someone else? Are you just trying to survive, you old rabbit you? Do we just fulfill our genetics? Maybe, you would you rather live like a rabbit from hell! Or, is it time to set some new goals that can help turn us into that 'thundering engine of hair and slobber!'

Another goal and action story: If there is a $100 bill across the room with your name on it, standing and talking to it won't help. Even yelling at it and telling it to, "Come!" won't help. If you want that $100, you must take some action. You must get out of your chair, go across the room and pick it up. You need to chase that bill as though it were a rabbit. If you start across the room and spend your time looking at the ceiling or out of the window or behind you, you'll never get to the $100 bill because you aren't focused on it. You don't know where it is and you can't see how to get there! All of our life successes have the same two components. Focus on the goal, set in concrete, taking action on our plans, set in sand, and voila! Yes, the rabbit is yours. You can have rabbit stew. You don't have to just eat rabbit pellets!! Do you want to be a 'thundering engine', or just 'hair and slobber'?

I know this has been a little silly, but it does have a point. Let's take charge of our lives from now on! If we don't do it, there are plenty of people out there who will and you may not like what they have planned for you. So, in review, put your goals in concrete; your plans in sand; use focus with action;

become a thundering engine, not hair and slobber; eat rabbit stew, not pellets!

Did you ever see such a clearly defined plan for success? You can thank your pets. They are our teachers!

Dr. J'isms

1. Are we just rabbits?

2. Are we, *thundering engines of hair and slobber*?

3. Set your goals in concrete, your plans in sand.

4. Eat rabbit stew, not rabbit pellets

5. Focus and action create *our* success!

FUN PAGE
Your Furry Interlude

1. Write down 3 emotions you would have if you were a *thundering engine of hair and slobber*.

2. Write down 3 emotions you would have if you were a rabbit.

3. Choose and write down 6 reasons you would prefer the emotions of list 1 or list 2. Then create them in your life!

Hannah in a *life happens* moment, chewing out of her dog bed.

Chapter 18
Recycling!

Recycling! What a great idea! You should do your part, please. What's the comment, "Do what you can with what you have!" However, I am referring to people who adopt pets from shelters, rescues or, perhaps, other people. These aren't puppies. Puppies have a clean slate for you to write upon. With puppies, you create what you want. With puppies, you create what you will have. So, if you have a pet from a puppy, you have what you created!

What we are talking about here are the pets that have a history. They have a past relationship somewhere, sometime with someone, or sadly, perhaps with no one. When adopted by us, the honeymoon starts! We love it! They love it! It's a new pet to share our life with. For the pet, it's a new place with new smells with a new pack and all joy, joy, joy.

THEN, the dog poops in the house or curls up to sleep on the couch or scratches a hole in the screen door after being left outside. It may turn his/her nose up at dog food or take their dog food out of their bowl and hide it around the house. They may jump up on your bed and relieve themselves! The list goes on and on and on.

We can't believe it! What we see as abnormal behavior, they see as normal. Suddenly, in an instant of time, the honeymoon is over and you are ready to take this BEAST back to where it came from. Divorce is everywhere! The dilemma: You saved this creature and want to succeed and you aren't. What a disappointment. Big bummer! Only sadness abounds when relationships (any relationships) spiral out of control, crash and burn. Is this the end? NO! Retraining can come to the rescue and make recycled relationships work. Training works wonders in relationships with dogs and with people!

So, the question is, "Why or how did this happen?" I have seen hundreds of successes and a only a few failures. What are the correlations between our pets and us? Well, one correlation is that your brain and this new dog's are identical when it comes to relationships, especially new relationships.

We have all been in previous relationships, whether personal, work or family. We may now be in new relationships that are struggling and we wonder why. Well, your dog has the answer. Think about it, our Border Collie brains love a routine. We train up our brains just like training a dog. We train our brains either on purpose or by default, but we do train them. Training is a daily occurrence. Again, we train either by choice or default. At least, until this moment, most of us have trained by default. The divorce rate in humans is the telltale sign for us. The high rate of euthanasia in shelters is the telltale sign for our pets.

Our relationships might be new, but our trained brain relationship habits are from our previous ones, the recent or even distant, past. The newly adopted dog's old habits, and our old habits, try to express themselves exactly as if we were in the old relationship. It's the same old movie in a different theatre! Again, it's that trained brain thing, dogs, cats or us. BUT this is a new relationship and all of the old behaviors just do not apply!

It may have been okay for you to relieve yourself on a bed in your old relationship, but with the bed in the new one, "NO! BAD DOG!" Remember, we ignore the bad behavior while praising the good behavior! Whatever gets the most emotional response becomes the future. It is normal for new dogs to apply their old behavior to a new situation and it can cause a lot of grief and frustration for those living in the new situation. Humans are no different. In fact, you could say that humans are exactly the same! Those divorce statistics indicate that there are a lot of old behaviors that help new relationships to 'spiral out of control, crash and burn.'

With a new relationship/job/task/career, we also vigorously apply the old behaviors onto the new situation. When I counsel clients about recycled dogs, I warn them that their new pet will try to use 'old' behavior in their 'new' home. They don't know anything else to do. Life has always been this way. It'll always be this way, right? You don't know anything else to do … right? Wrong! However, this is normal, normal and normal for all of us.

Recap

Using old behavior patterns in a new situation is normal, but it seldom creates peace and harmony. Old behavior in new situations should be expected, but it needs to be adjusted in a positive way. Don't tolerate the bad behavior but understand that it will take some training to make the situation fulfill the expected joy. Where we err is in thinking that they are so cute, we let them get away with old behavior in the new situation and it only gets worse very quickly. Validating old behavior only makes the new relationship crash and burn quickly and the honeymoon is over! Some honeymoons are very short, for pets or for people!

I used to ask clients that had recently married, when they came in for their next office visit, "Are you still married?" I always expected an affirmative response. Lately, I had two clients, less than 90 days from their marriage, say, "No, we had it annulled!" So, I don't go there anymore, but it did make me ponder this topic about recycling and your pets.

It would be at this point that women decide I'm talking only about men and their behavior! BUT all behavior is actually a gender-neutral topic.

Really, men and dogs aren't the same ... really! A woman can teach a man to come, sit, heel, stay, wash, iron, vacuum, cook and take out the trash. If his mother didn't do it before the age of three, you are doomed. Be happy if he learns to put the toilet seat down! All of us have these same tendencies in recycled relationships because our brains are Border Collies! In other words, our brains respond the way they were trained. With the new relationships or a new situation, our brains need to be retrained and it takes some time.

Recycled dogs have to be trained to their new home using the same principles. You must praise the good, ignore the bad and protect the house in some way until they are trained. Many dogs (perhaps men, too) have been trained badly but usually just have a lack of training. When this is the case, you are just watching their genetics or old habits running wild on default. Their behavior needs modification to fit the new circumstances. Recycled relationships do not have to crash and burn over and over and over again. They can last and last and last. They can fulfill expectations! However, it may require some commitment and persistence on everyone's part.

Here's the point to this little *recycling* story. If you would train a dog to fit into your life, why wouldn't you train your own brain when you are in a new circumstance, job or relationship. Few people realize that responding in the 'old relationship' way to a situation in a new relationship is seldom correct, constructive or comforting, even though it's a normal thing to do. Hmmm, I like that C.C.C. thing – Correct, constructive, comforting!

We should really evaluate ourselves when we are in a new job/relationship/task or career. We should ask ourselves, "Is what I feel like doing, what I used to do or what seems most comfortable to me the correct response now?"

Like a dog, the only control we have over our lives is how we respond to what occurs. There is nothing, nada, zero, zilch, else that we can control. Most of us spend our lives worrying about things that we are unable to control and will probably never happen. We are unable to control things like the weather, disasters, and drunkards on the road, the economy or the latest cancer that is lurking in your body. When "life happens" in our recycled relationships, we can overcome it with retraining! No excuses anymore!

Dr. J'isms

1. Recycling: Positive results all around!
2. Our brains/dog brains need new training with new relationships.
3. The honeymoon always ends.
4. Expectations can be fulfilled.
5. Praise the good.
6. Ignore the bad.
7. If you can train your dog, you can train your brain!
8. Control how we react to "life happens!"

FUN PAGE
Your Recycling

1. List 3 items from your past relationships, job or career that didn't work in a new environment because of old behaviors. Ex. "I thought I could _____, but boy, that didn't work."

2. List 3 items that aren't working well in your life right now.

3. List two ways for each item in 2 in which you can develop new ways to resolve the 'recycling' problem and then do it! Now, create them in your life!

Dad sharing Hannah's chair

Chapter 19

The Oooooooops Syndrome, or Why We Love Dogs

In recycled pet training, the first thing we should do is to recognize that some behavior is no longer appropriate. I call that the oooooops syndrome. Until our recycled pet (or us) use an old behavior in a new situation, we don't know it exists. Until we realize that the old behavior is lurking in there, from our past, wired into our brain and waiting to jump out, we can't make progress. After we use the old behavior in a new situation, it usually causes chaos. When this happens, life is not so fun and we begin multiple visits to our counseling person. With a pet, it should be your veterinarian.

OOOOOOPS, our rescued pet isn't working out. My new relationship is a mistake. Life, in general, sucks. Life can be a vacuum cleaner, or if you are British, "Life is a Hoover!" What a mistake I made! Now I have to start all over again with yet another relationship or rescued pet. WRONG!

If we haven't learned anything the first time around, starting over again only recreates the nightmare. How many times do you want to live in the same loop, the same loop, the same loop? All we need to do is some 'in the moment' training, whether it's the new pet or them or ourselves. Notice that I said, "Some training, not a lot of training!" Children can be taught not to run all over the exam room, rummaging through the trash, screaming at the pets, playing with the computer keys, crawling across the counter tops to get to the otoscope or ophthalmoscope, or throwing their stuffed toys into the aquarium. Really, they can be taught this, really. It only requires some training! Your recycled dog can make a wonderful companion and you can adjust to a new human relationship or task or career with "some training!" Really!

The reason relationships are complicated is because we believe they should be. It's what we have been taught. It's how we have been trained. Remember, for dogs and us, perception is reality. Relationships for our pets are simple!

Consider this. Men love dogs because a dog accepts them as they are. Dogs don't want to change them. Dogs love to be with them wherever they are or go. Dogs don't care how dirty their car or truck is, whether or not they have showered or smell like beer and cigars. When men come home, the dog jumps up barking and roars around the house announcing that Dad's home, the man is back, the pack leader is in the building! You are da' man, you are da' man!! Yes, dogs recognize that the man is the pack leader and men know hero worship when they see it! Hero worship works with men! Men love their dogs. Dogs just want to be next to him. They want to be with him and do his thing. What a man sees reflected in his dog's eyes is pure unadulterated acceptance and non-judgmental adulation. Most men will do anything for their dog. There is a lesson here for any man's human companion. There are reasons behind the statement, "I think you care more for that dog than you do for me!" Let's see. Perception is reality?

Women love dogs because they can train a dog not to make a mess in the house. A dog never leaves clothes lying around that smell. A dog acts like it cares about what a woman is saying. A dog is always happy, really happy, to see her. Oh, look, it's Mom, spelled food, food and food!! A dog really just wants to be with her, share her space, just lay it's head on her lap while she reads and drinks her hot chocolate. Women can train dogs to come when they want and to do what they want, when they want! A dog or a cat is the ultimate companion for a woman. They usually rank higher than the humans in their lives.

I have always believed that if a woman can get the same look in her eyes that a man sees in his dog's eyes, that woman will have the life she always wanted to have with a man. I know it is sexist and gendered, but if we would all watch and study a dog's behavior in how it interacts with humans, there are things to learn. Keep reading, it also applies to men!

If a man would watch how a dog defers to a woman's opinion and behavior, he would be a highly satisfied male. Both males and females need to observe the body posture and watch what a dog does after the man has been home for a few minutes. Watch what your pet does when Mom comes home. See what kind of a perception (reality?) the male has about his relationship with his dog. Watch how a dog responds to what a woman says to it. There is some value in realizing that if you treat a man like a dog, you know, come, sit, heel and stay, you'll both be very happy! Oh, and if you are a man? If you want a great relationship with a woman: watch how your dog reacts to its woman…. you could learn some new behaviors! The perception of being loved or cared about is the ticket to success.

Ok, so that's fairly facetious and superficial, but a lot of women have said to their dog, "At least you care about what I want! There are no conditions on your love." A friend's first wife told him that he was nicer to his dogs than to her, but he said that she didn't love him like his dogs did! I've heard variations on this statement with both genders dozens of times. While we are thinking about these things, 'da' dog is really thinking, "Yep, some food is about to happen! I love this pack!

My only point is that dogs have the ability to keep genders, identities and most personalities happy. Pets have talent and skills we can all learn and should apply! Most humans can't even keep one relationship intact over the long term. We all love our pets and will fight for them in a divorce. There is hope for us! Watching the behavior of your pet will show you how your genetic (Border Collie) brain functions. By applying what we learn by watching our pets and acting on it, we can move forward with what we want in our life and relationships!

Dr. J'isms

1. Relationships can be wonderful.

2. Men love dogs.

3. Women love dogs.

4. Watching dogs can show us how to act with others.

5. If we can train a dog, we can train ourselves!

FUN PAGE
Oooooops, or Loving Each Other

1. List 3 times in the last year when ooooops occurred in your life.

2. Write what you learned from each event.

3. Write down why you like your pet and your significant other. Notice how the lists are similar or not. Choose the best list for your attitude of the future.

Dinner!!

Hannah

Dickon, Tucker and Pippin!

Chapter 20
Treats! The Gender Thing

Let's talk about treats for dogs and learn something about us. It's that table food or human snack food thing. Commonly, in an exam room when telling a female client that her dog could lose a few pounds to hit the ideal canine body score of 3 on a scale of one to 5, she blames her husband. The weight issue is due to the treats that her husband, her fiance, her son or her retired male neighbor that feeds their pet that creates the problem. Never, yes, and I mean never, is it the husband, son, boyfriend (note: all male genders) saying, "It's my wife or girlfriend or fiancé or Mom or sister that is feeding the extra treats.

Yes, especially since I am a male, I know that the tendency or overwhelming urge is for males to share treats and food with the family pets. Adulation or hero worship makes men want to give gifts, share life, have fun and create security. Human males would share more than just their food and snacks with their significant others if they had the same relationship with them as they do with their dogs.

In my experience, women are definitely much more structured when it comes to the topic of food, at least for their pets. It is only my opinion, but it's what I've observed for years. Yes, it is cat food for cats, and men eat what they want no matter what their physician or their partner recommends! Well, okay, maybe only most men. Except for the calories, table food is as good for dogs as it is for us. Our food is fairly dense in calories, tastes good and can easily cause weight gain in a pet. They will also never want their dog food again!

In these situations, I recommend that women say to their husbands, sons and male friends that they can feed all the fruits and veggies they want as a treat for their dogs. These contain fiber, vitamins, minerals, very few calories and our pets usually eat them. An exception is grapes or raisins. They can cause kidney damage in some dogs. Everything else sounds like a good idea, right?

Ha! The looks I have seen in the eyes of the women. Seriously, I'm glad it's not directed at me. The look says: "You've got to be kidding. I can't even get my (*insert male's name*) to eat fruits and veggies. How can you possibly believe they'll share those with our dog?" They usually think I'm just being funny, so I tell them that I know it's nearly hopeless. Honestly, if a man eats chips, his pet eats chips. If a man eats popcorn with butter and salt, so does his pet. Is this a sexist attitude? Sure, but in summary, you should at least try to limit the quantity of all table food for your pet, except for fruits and veggies.

Men are men, no matter what their age. Dogs are always wonderful companions, no matter what human gender owns them. Repeating that we must praise for the good, ignore the bad and we have peace in the home.

Some pets are defective, like some men or women and must be dealt with on the, "Protect yourself from the jerks!" category. If you think you have an animal that may fall into the "jerks" category, and there are some, call your local veterinarian and get it sorted out. If you are living with a human jerk, get it sorted out. Life is too short to put up with Mr., Mrs., Ms. or Pet Misery until the cows come home!

Because our relationships with our pets fall into that category under love, much like it is with humans, I had to redefine how I viewed and treated many humans. Our relationships should fall into that pet kind of love with everyone around us. I can't say I've always succeeded but at least I have been making the attempt for a long time. I'm a lot closer to using the pet kind of love today about you than I was years ago. Because of your pets and what they have taught me, I know that next year I'll be closer than today. It's never too late to find and practice the attitude embodied in that "pet kind of love." This brings us to our next topic!

Dr. J'isms

1. Dog food for dogs.

2. Cat food for cats.

3. Cow food for cows.

4. Human food for humans.

5. Women are structured.

6. Men are loosey-goosey.

7. Get your jerks sorted out.

FUN PAGE
Treats And Your Gender

1. List all the food and treats your pet gets to have during a day.

2. List all the food and treats you get to have during the same day.

3. Compare the lists and see if either can be improved with healthier choices. Then eat off the new list!

Snuggle love always works

Chapter 21
Love, Baby! Yes, Love!

Love humans? Love humans? You've got to be kidding! Yes, please, it brings out the best in them and in you. Look at what our pets do for us by loving us first. Our behavior changes for the better when we are around animals. When we see a pet smiles break out, stress is lifted, good memories and endorphins flood your brain. Life in the presence of a loving pet is always better.

Numerous studies have documented the positive impact of the human-animal bond. It took me a few years in practice to find out that if you can love your dog or cat or horse, you can love humans. More importantly, if you can love a pet, you can learn to love yourself. It's certainly okay to be content with your life as it is but you should never be complacent. If you aren't moving forward, you are moving backwards. Be happy where you are, but always be moving into your future!

By accepting you as you are is the way your pets get you to be the wonderful people you are, at least with them. A prayer I've heard people use in public settings is, "Lord, please help me become the person my pet thinks I am!" A similar statement I have used in recent years is that, "When it comes to humans, you just have to love them. Protect yourself from the jerks, but love everyone else." That is what your pets have taught me about the human race. We must accept people the way they are. We should love 'em the way we find 'em.! We can let them know they are okay in our books and then watch the relationships build. That's how your pet treats you and you love your pets because of it!

It is commonly known that if a person can abuse an animal, they will abuse human beings. Most serial killers and bullies begin their "careers' by abusing animals. Animal abuse is part of their profile. These individuals are either genetically defective or a human disaster that requires major intervention to have a chance of redemption as a contributor to society. Is that dramatic sounding enough? It's pretty close to the facts.

I know we live in these bodies, usually being run on default by our Border Collie brains. However, we do get to choose our behavior toward others, including these wonderful four-legged sentient beings that live with us on this spinning top we call Earth. These animals think you are pretty special. I've seen it in their eyes and tails (if they have one) when you walk into our office with them. Because of what I've seen in their eyes, I have slowly, grudgingly, over decades, agreed with what they have taught me: You are pretty special. Yes, they taught me to care about you and to accept myself.

The humans that hate and wound, for whatever protective reason they may have, have little redeeming value as a life form in the scheme of things. They fall into that category of jerks and drive (seemingly) a lot of cars on the highways. Their treatment should include spending time locked up with a pet so they can learn about life. On second thought, no pet should have to suffer this.

You are probably beginning to understand that there are several themes running through this short book. These themes are relationships, consistency, unlimited potential, Border Collie brain training, men are like dogs, women are in charge and a look at our lives as dogs see us. Can you see a common thread running through all of these?

Cool, Dude and Joe Cool are phrases from the past that have different connotations (or none, if you are young) for each of us. But, can't you begin to realize that you really are "cool"? I have heard it quoted that 2 out of 3 people have low self-esteem. I am not qualified to comment on self-esteem issues, except for what I see in all the animals I observe. Animals generally exhibit great self-esteem. They like themselves! They like their lives. They like you!

Our low self-esteem issues seem to be only in our eyes. It is not reflected in the eyes of our pets. It's not reflected in the eyes of your pets. People have had a lot of opinions about me over the years and they generally expressed themselves. It was difficult not to label myself according to their opinions. I have learned that just because someone calls me a baseball bat, it doesn't make me one. However, our pets see something in us that we can't or won't see in ourselves. Maybe it's time for us to start looking!

In reviewing this manuscript, Maureen Cummins, a recently retired high school teacher and co-founder of *Second Chance Animal Rescue Society* (SCARS- www.scarsusa.com) with her husband, Terry, submitted this next paragraph. Their experiences with rescued and recycled dogs has led them to some very accurate insights.

Maureen wrote, "Isn't it time you took your pet seriously and realized that you are, indeed, a fantastic person. If it were not true, your pet would not think so. Animals are smart. Just watch a dog shrink and put his tail between his legs around a jerk. Watch a normally loving dog curl his lip when an abusive, rude person is around. Why would you doubt their opinion with regard to yourself? If they love you, it is because you are lovable. The end. Period. Full stop. I have known people, primarily single women, tell me they judge their boyfriends by the way their dog responds to them." Thank you, Maureen.

Seeing ourselves through our pet's eyes is a new concept. I know that they see good things in you. I didn't see these things until I watched them interact with you in my office and exam rooms over the decades. These critters knew something that took me years to learn, "You have worth. You make their day. You are the light in their life. Without you, their life would be dim. You are their whole focus and the center of their universe." Substitute "I or me" for "You" and reread the last few lines that are in quotation marks. The theme that runs through these comments is how we should view ourselves. This knowledge gives us the capacity to go forward with our lives. To go forward with what you want in your life. To go forward leaving the baggage behind. Now is the time to adjust, focus on your future and go!

When we make eye contact with our pets, they look at us and their tail begins to move, their eyebrows go up and their body language says, "Hey, what are we going to do? I'm ready to follow you. Lead or get out of the way but let's go!" We love that interaction, yet many of us can't look ourselves in the eye in a mirror and feel the same way. You should try it. It'll feel silly or stupid, but you'll be amazed at what you'll see or not see. Quit judging yourself for the past. Everyone's lives have mistakes. Go look in a mirror and look yourself in the eye today! If you really work at it, you will find what your dog or cat sees in you. If you look for what makes their life and their opinion of you so good, you'll eventually find it in yourself. Find out what they see. What is it they like that inspires them to get out of their warm spot to come over and say, "Hi, isn't life great? Aren't you great? Is your lap available?" They see it in our eyes, so it must be there. Go look for it until you can say to the eyes in the mirror, "Hi! Isn't life great and the future exciting!"

Your Border Collie brain with all of its self imposed conditions, self condemnations, memories of the past and uneasy vision for the future will have to yield to what your pet sees in your eyes. It may take some training. It may take practice. It may take time. It may take commitment, consistency and persistence.

Today is the beginning of your future. Your future is a blank sheet of paper that only you get to write on. Don't use the Border Collie brain default button, make choices! Pick a new program! Make your dog or cat or significant other or children or parents or friends or most importantly, you, proud of you. Your pets love you the way you are, so keep looking in the mirror until you can love yourself the way you are and then you will be ready for your dynamically exciting, possibilities unlimited, choice driven future!

Dr. Doug Jernigan

Dr. J'isms

1. If you can love your pets, you can love yourself.
2. Pets have great self-esteem.
3. Look in a mirror to see what your pet sees.
4. You have worth!
5. Pets accept us as we are.
6. Accept ourselves as we are.
7. No default buttons, just our choices creating our future!

FUN PAGE
Loving Yourself

1. Make a list of 3 things you do well. Ex. Cook or clean or laugh.

2. Write down why you do list 1 items well and how you feel when you do it.

3. Apply the answers found in 2 to the rest of your life!

Hannah and her cloudy day *sunny spot*, one of her vents!

Chapter 22
Changing The Unchangeable

What is it! What! When a dog sees something that does not compute, the hackles rise, it's posture becomes alert, the ears go up and forward and the eyes focus right down the nose onto the 'does not compute' thing. Remember, your Border Collie brain part is quicker than your logic, your higher centers. M.R.I. studies measure the difference. You will always react emotionally before your logic kicks in. We feel before we think. It's a survival strategy built into your body to keep you alive! It's automatic, it happens. You will always be running before you know what you are running from!

You and your dog are identical in that respect. You just have a lot more *logical* ability built into you than your pet does. It also gives us the ability to worry about things that are not in our 'now.' Dogs pretty much live in the 'now.' I think they only live for the future as it gets close to dinner time! When you are home and food might be available. You are home and your lap might be available with an afghan for warmth and a nap. You are away from home, so where is the nearest sunny spot, what's going on outside the deck door, what was that noise, what is in my reality 'now.' This is where our pets live. We need to live here. It's called the NOW!

When you live this way, your stress disappears and you can focus better on what's occurring now like, "Oooooh, aaaaah, time for a nap!" You will usually work on one task at a time and it will make your memory or recall, more efficient. Studies have proven this about memory. With increased efficiency, you can find more *sunny spots* in your day. Don't we want our life to be dog life good?

The reason I bring this up is that most of us focus on things we cannot change. We spend our life trying to change the unchangeable! What is unchangeable? Our dog would say the time he/she eats is unchangeable. They have no control over it. You do. They would say that the weather is unchangeable. They can't make the sunny spots appear. They have to find them! You get the drift.

Because of our greater capacity to think, we worry about things that we can't control. This lack of control creates stress, anxiety and disappointment. If we can't control the unchangeable, we certainly can't change it. When was the last time you worried about what the weather would do to your plans? Could you stop the weather? Could you make the sunny spots go somewhere else or come to you on command? No, we can't control the weather or the sunny spots, but we can plan around the weather.

I greatly admire my younger daughter. As a bright, enthusiastic, a high S (helping) C (detailed, list maker) she does what she wants in her career and if she comes up against things that she can't change, she does something else. She keeps her overhead low, her material possessions few, lives in the 'now' and doesn't hesitate to change what she does. The unchangeable is never a hindrance to her happiness or her life choices! I am learning this lesson. It applies to all of us. Our pets show us the way by living in the now.

I have friends whose idea of a great time is to watch the weather channel! Some people feel the only thing worse would be to watch a fishing show or golf! Well, sometimes, I'll do the weather and golf, but never fishing! A few years ago I was listening to a friend explaining their worries about some events that were coming in their life. It was like watching the weather channel. The realization was stunning! Every single thing he was worrying about, he had no control over. The worst part of that whole event was realizing that I do the same thing!

His thought patterns were no different than mine. He was letting a lot of little things make him miserable days before the event. Planning is one thing, being freaky about things we can't control is another. In fact, your dog would say, "Who cares if there is no sunny spot today, I'll find a heat vent to lie on. I know the vent is only temporary! The sunny spots will be back!" Human behaviorists and health care professionals would tell you that this is a healthy life skill worth learning and using. The lesson is here for all of us to learn and use. It comes from your pet!

Many of us live our lives sadly. No, we don't live sad lives. We just live life sadly. In fact, to others, your lives look outstanding! But for many of us, the glass is half empty, not half full. In contrast, for our pets, the glass is just a place to get a drink of water. They have no value judgments or comparisons to make them miserable. For many of us, our glass is half full of misery and we can't see anything else. It can go on like this for days, weeks, months, years, decades or a lifetime. It can be changed and it can be changed now! Use your 'glass' only to get a drink of water!

When we talked about goals, we said, "Goals in concrete, plans in sand." Our goals do need to be something that is not changeable and they are controllable. We can't control the weather and how it will affect our plans because we can't change it. Spending your day 'thinking' your hair color from red to black or straight to curly won't change it. Getting a box of dye and streaking it up will change it, but that takes action. Action is always the key.

Planning an outdoor event in Kansas needs to have an indoor back up plan any time of the year. Remember that the only control we have in our lives is how we respond to what occurs. When did we hear this before? Does *life happen* during our days?

To your dog, if the sunny spot moves, they don't just sit in the same spot and wish it would come back across the room to where they are lying. They get up and chase it! They know that if you want a new sunny spot in your life and circumstances, you have to find it. It won't find you. Lying in the dark and cold won't make it happen. You'll just be dark and cold. Whose life are we talking about anyway? You have to take some action to stay in the sunny spots.

That's the lesson from your pet. Stay in the now, don't worry about what you can't change, respond to what is happening and know that if the sun isn't out, it's only temporary! Find a heat vent! Get fired up; don't just be waiting to die! If a dog feels fine, they assume they are healthy. If a human feels fine, we know that we are about to come down with cancer, bankruptcy, auto wrecks, airplane crashes, tornadoes, hurricanes, blizzards, robbery, terrorism and mayhem (whatever that is). We can't control the future, but we can plan for it and we can create it. Set your goals, make your plans and respond when that 'life happens' thing occurs. Live in your sunny spots daily. Use a vent if you need to temporarily. Act *for* the future, not in *fear* of it. Have concrete goals, sandy plans and create the life you want! Haven't our pets taught us some interesting things?

Ok, a short Hannah vent story. Hannah had excellent hearing. In the winter, when the forced air furnace kicks in, she listens, and then goes in search of her favorite floor vent. She likes several, but usually it's the one that is closest to wherever we are. She sits near or on the vent and lets the heat waft over her. Her eyes close, her ears flap a little, she sighs and slumbers. Life is warm sleeping dog good!

When the season changes into summer and the fan kicks in, she listens and then goes in search of her favorite floor vent. Only now, the air conditioner is on and only icy air greets her. She will sit there and let this cold air blow into her face and ears. She sits there and turns her head back and forth. She lets her ears flap a little, squints her eyes and eventually she'll get up and leave. BUT she has done this her whole life! During the summer months she will even *retry* the vent on the next cooling cycle to see if the heat is back. It isn't. As I'm writing this, she is checking out the vent and it's July! The air conditioner has been on for weeks! My wife and I always have a great chuckle about how, "she just doesn't get it!"

We laugh, but how many of us exhibit the same behavior with the 'floor vents' in our lives? Things change. Life happens. But if our *air vents* have gone cold, going back to the same air vent expecting warm air is a waste of our time. For us to be comfortable, icy air requires different behavior. What was good and soothing is now frigid creating stress and anxiety. We don't have to keep going back and getting chilled. We can look at our lives and see if it's time to find a new source of warmth and validation. Hannah may not get it, but we certainly can.

Am I talking about relationships, careers, jobs, or habits? Sure, all of the above! If these situations, over which we have no control, are suddenly 'cold air' for us, it's time for action! Don't just sit there and let your ears freeze!

In the next chapter, I'll show you how to 'find your own way' from a cold air vent to a new warm one!

Dr. J'isms

1. Live like your pet. Live in the **now**!

2. Chase your sunny spots.

3. A cloudy day is temporary, so look for a heat vent.

4. Goals in concrete! Plan around the unchangeable.

5. Control is responding when life happens.

6. It takes action to find a new heat source.

FUN PAGE
Changing Into *Now*!

1. Make a list of 3 things you worry about.

2. Evaluate whether or not you can control list 1 and write it down.

3. If you cannot control this, throw it out of your mind. If you can, set some goals in concrete with sandy plans and go looking for the sunny spots in these items!

Looking back at the *leeeaaaning* deck door!

Chapter 23
Finding Our Own Way ... With Joss

Joss was our Border Collie. She was so smart that she housetrained quckly, but in the end it was we, not she, who had to be housetrained. As a puppy, Joss quickly learned that when we took her out, she was to go 'business.' Yes, I follow my own training advice. Inside our home, she was a little flaky on her training and had a few accidents because she just wouldn't let us know when she wanted out. It was frustrating for all three of us. However, she was very obedient and very efficient with her business when we took her out. While she loved to please us, we felt that she just didn't quite get it. Remember, this was our Border Collie, a proud member of the smartest breed and before

Hannah joined us!

One evening we noticed, as we were watching television, that she was leaning up against the door to our deck. She would look us in the eye and then leeeaaan up against the deck door that leads into the back yard, the 'business' yard.

Before we go on, I have to tell you about Border Collie eyes. Border Collie eyes, when turned on you, change you into sheep. You may be very odd looking sheep but you are still sheep. You will even feel like sheep. Border Collie eyes will stop you in your tracks. Border Collie eyes lock onto other eyes like a military sniper onto his or her target. Communication is complete. There is a task at hand. The Border Collie is in charge, so get it together and pay attention!

Having felt like sheep with Joss before, we looked at each other and wondered what in the world she was doing. She was really acting rather strange. You would swear that she had a *don't you guys get it?* look in her eye. Her eyes would 'snap' at us and then she would leeeaaan on the door. Then her eyes would snap back at us and she would leeeaaan on the door. She wanted to go out. The deck door wasn't our business door but she was sending us a message. After she figured how to communicate with us, dummies that we were, housetraining was simple. We still do not speak dog very well, but we're getting there. In the nearly 13 years we had Joss with us, she taught us a lot of *dog*!

Since we weren't getting it, Joss had to find her own way to let us know when she wanted out. Finding our own way when the 'normal' things aren't working is what Joss has to show us. We are never lost. We can always find our way. We can always figure it out. We all have Border Collie brains! When you are in a situation that you can't figure out, "Let the Joss be with you!"

Joss would use her eyes in other ways, but the principle was always the same. As I said, the eyes are where Border Collies live! If she wanted to play with her toys, she would bring it to us, drop it and then position herself to look right into our eyes. It was in those moments that we would feel a little bit like a lamb, ewe or ram.

After eye contact, she would move her eyes slowly to the toy and then, snap! back to your eyes. Then a slow eye movement to the toy and then, snap! back to your eyes. If you didn't respond she would up her game to a yip or a bark. If we were really ignoring her request, as a last resort, she would paw at your leg to demand that you play with her. If we told her "Wait" she would go lie down with a flump and a sigh. Life could be so boring! She was sweet, obedient and knew how to communicate what she wanted. We really miss her.

What is the lesson for us? Can we learn how to communicate when people aren't 'getting' it? Can you find your own way, even with the dummies in your life that don't speak your language well? The answers to your life lie within you. Joss knew when she wanted out. She knew what she wanted to do. She found her own way to get it done. Joss taught us that if we know what we want, we are able to find our own way to get it done. Paths that others have used to get what you want might work for you, but they may not. Your path is the correct one for you. If you want answers for the situations in your life, like Joss, you can find them!

In our lives, we run into circumstances that are strange to us. They just don't make sense. These are things that are out of our comfort zone. These may be things we don't know how to deal with based on our past experiences or genetic input.

Dogs, when confronting these types of situations just sit back and observe. They will watch what's going on and decide how they should respond. They watch, make choices and act. Sit, watch, choose and act. It's a great strategy for humans. It's a strategy few of us use. Using it brings wonderful results. When things seem to be going out of control and nothing makes sense just sit back, observe and then act. Seldom do dogs just turn tail and run or attack unless they are really threatened. So, the key from out pets is to observe and then act. The only control for us is how we respond to what happens.

If a dog is a D type of dog, they may just aggressively challenge the situation until they can get a handle on it, but usually they observe and then take action. Some dogs may have evident stress, their ears may be down, their tail (if they have one) may be tucked under and their body will be turned sideways without making eye contact. But, even turned sideways, they're observing, deciding on action. We should do so well.

We are usually good on observing, but taking action or knowing when to take action isn't our strong suit. Humans are pretty good at opting out, going emotionally numb just going along with the crowd (pack), or slowly disappearing into the dust of life. While these are actions, they are usually based on self-protective pain or feel good Border Collie brain responses. We should make our decisions based on observation. We really need to use our higher logical centers to evaluate, decide and then act. At that point in time, we can be confident that our decision is based on what we want ... not just what we feel.

Our feelings are there to protect us, not to take us into our future! Feelings are hooked up with our Border Collie brains. We can use them to propel us into our future, but if left to run on default, they are designed to protect us, to keep us where we are. So, any time you feel like things are out of control, just think of yourself as a dog trotting through the country side pausing long enough to consider the new thing and then act. All stress is temporary. There will always be a new meadow at the end of the field to explore!

Like dogs, we perceive the world through our eyes, ears, nose, touch and taste. To a dog, the nose is sense #1. For us, our vision is #1. Dogs are mildly nearsighted, but do see color at some level. From a distance, your own dog may growl at you until he or she can either smell you or you get close enough to see you more clearly. In new or stressful situations, we humans are reacting from our Border Collie brain. Using our logical higher centers makes life much less stressful. We are in control only of how we respond to what is occurring around us. Dogs do this instinctively. We have to learn it. Come, Sit, Heel, Down, Stay and Learn it!! Take the time to observe, decide, then act. If you act more like a dog, your life will be less stressful, be more fun, and more successful.

Medical diagnosticians take a lot of abstract information and distill it down to its essence creating a diagnosis. There is a lot of information to consider in these chapters and by the time we get to the end, you will have a cut to the chase *diagnosis* provided by your pets on how to have a most rewarding life of your choosing! As we were with Joss, you'll 'get it' for your life and future!

Dr. Doug Jernigan

Dr. J'isms

1. All the answers to your life lie within you
2. Communication takes many forms.
3. *Dummies* can learn.
4. New situations require observation and action.
5. Going *catatonic* in life is a choice.
6. Your life is your abstract information.
7. Your *diagnosis* creates your future.
8. Action is the treatment for whatever ails you!

FUN PAGE
Changing Into *Now*!

1. List 3 events from your past where you felt really out of your comfort zone.

2. Write down if you *reacted* or if you observed, decided and then acted for each event.

3. Write down how you can observe, decide and then act daily in your life. It will become a great habit.

Need I say more?

Chapter 24

The Post Person Syndrome

My wife doesn't really have to love me. I just need the perception that she does! As you know, perception is reality. Or you could say, "Reality is what we perceive it to be." In Shakespearean play this (my paraphrase) appeared. "No event is of itself good or bad, only thinking makes it so!" In other words, perception is reality.

To house or yard dogs, perception is truly reality. Who you see as a mail carrier, your pet sees as a potential intruder. We see delivery people as helping us. Your pet sees them as a threat to be dealt with. When we see them continuing on their daily rounds, our dogs see them as retreating from their ferocious response to their territorial threat. The enemy has been chased away.

Why do our pet's perceptions of these events vary so much from ours? Here is how their perception is created. It is their reality and it is as valid to them as ours is to us.

When the post person arrives (pick UPS, FEDEX or any other daily delivery service) most dogs will react in a territorially protective way. However, if they are a high "I," they'll just want to party with the new guy or gal at the door. But for most dogs, it usually goes like this!

The truck with the distinctive engine noise drives up, knock, knock, (we all know who's there!) ding, dong, then bark-growl-bark-bounce-snarl-bark-bark … bark, bark, bark, bark, until a few minutes after they have left. Then the dog will cock his or her head, look around, give a last snort of derision or satisfaction and go on with his or her life.

The next day, it starts again, about the same time and your home's protector performs again with the same results. The next day, about the same time, it happens again, only this time your home protection dog is becoming a furry frothy-mouthed beast and is much more satisfied after the event!

The event is escalating because they keep coming back and obviously need more convincing to leave! This cycle continues over time until the inside of your door is scarred and needs protection from your protector. Your furry protection agent is flying around the house, window to window, door to door with gnashing of teeth and howls of aggression (or is it joy?). Does any of this sound familiar around within your home? Right now, I'm talking about your dog. You'll be next.

As we know, your four legged ferocious furry protection agent has a perception of reality that differs from yours. The first time this confrontation occurred, your dog was a protection agent. Instinct and genetics were working correctly. Territorial protection is an instinct. They bark-growl-bark and guess what? She or he chases off (read that as *scares* away) the potential intruder, your post person. Perception as reality! The next day it happens again and again, success! But they keep coming back. Each day your dog needs to get more expressive with that trespasser so they will get the message, but they don't. Each day, they get *scared away*, each day they come back for a new lesson in protection and get *scared away*. This is your dog's perception of a routine mail delivery.

Is it reality? It is for your home protection agent. Eventually, usually years later, the post person will show up and your pet won't leave the sunny spot to do anything about it. They think they have trained the post person to leave on their own. Your pets will be lying in the sun when they hear the distinctive engine noises, the ding-dong and think, "There's that stupid post person again, he or she never learns!" I mean no disrespect to post people but that summarizes what most dogs think about you and why they would just as soon bite you as look at you. You are an intruder that just doesn't get it.

Now, in defense of post people, I know that many of you make wonderful friendships with the dogs on your routes. You have gone the extra mile by making a friend of a potential foe. The wise ones of you know that if you make a friend of a foe, you have a friend for life. However, with dogs, if you make a foe of a friend, they will never forget it. Not much different than we humans, eh?

Ok, let's talk about you! Can you think of anything in your life that fits what we just saw? I'll grant you that the aggressive attitude is typical of only a small part of humanity, but what about the perception as reality part. If we think it's real, our Border Collie brain really doesn't care if it's factual or not!

Some examples to get you thinking, "If they aren't Christians, they must be bad people. If they are Christians, they must be bigots. Being gay is a choice, not genetic, and they need to be discriminated against. Being gay is genetically based and they should have the same rights as everyone else. All politicians are in it for themselves. Most politicians are altruistic and want to do the right thing by creating a win-win situation. Used car dealers are dishonest. Used car dealers are great people and honest. Evolution is a theory and is bad science. Intelligent design is scientific and should be taught in schools. Religion and God is the same thing. God has nothing to do with religion." Your perception of these topics and everything else in your life is your reality. Can you see how this can affect our life, relationships and future?

I think you get the drift. Our perceptions create our reality and our brains don't care if it's factual. Your pet's perception of reality is its reality. In the same way, your reality is only your perception. If you want to change your reality, you must change your perceptions. If you cut to the chase, your perceptions are what you believe.

Well, your pet doesn't care what you believe. That's why we love them. Your pet doesn't care about what you perceive as real. Your pet doesn't see good or bad…only different. To your pet, the facts don't count. You wouldn't try to convince your pet that the world is flat, would you, even if it's popular today? Our pets don't care what our beliefs or perceptions are. They just accept us. You accept your pet's belief systems as they are. The attitude of accepting us the way we are is why we love our pets. Why shouldn't we have the same accepting attitude and respect for each other and our beliefs?

We accept our pets as they are. Our pets accept us as we are. Maybe we should adopt our pet's attitude and accept others (humans) as they are? It's a healthy thought. Stop judging. If your pet wouldn't care, why should you? This attitude keeps our pets happy. This attitude will keep you happy. Understand that perceptions are reality and accept others as they are Do your own thing. Sleep in a sunny spot, snoop under the couch, eat some bunny bon-bon's, but don't try to force others to do your thing! Reasoned discourse with mutual respect for each other's perception based realities is healthy. Applying this might create a better world for you and for those whose lives you touch! It works for dogs and cats, that's why you love them.

Dr. J'isms

1. Perception is reality to dogs.

2. Perception is reality for our *Border Collie* brains.

3. Perception is reality if we don't have the facts.

4. Perception is reality.

5. Your reality is perfect for you, please, keep it to yourself.

6. Acceptance trumps judgment and creates peace.

7. A peaceful life will grow success.

Before I close this chapter, there is topic that is important for your pet and you that is in the same context as the post person syndrome. We are all going to grow older. If we are fortunate, we'll remain healthy to a very old age. As I said previously, we are seeing animals attaining much older ages in greater numbers and remaining in better health than ever before. What we haven't discussed is how humans and animals perceive age related changes. There is a difference. As we grow older, we realize that we are losing our hearing, our vision is changing, our run becomes a walk and events that used to ring our bell don't even get a thought from us anymore. We know we are getting older. We are changing. We know it's usually for the better, but it's always older. Dogs and cats, however, perceive these changes totally differently.

Like us, as our pet's age, their vision changes as their lenses become more dense. They develop cataracts, actually called nuclear sclerosis, and their world begins to become more hazy, blurry and dim. In the early stages of vision change, clients notice that their pet's depth perception is changing. Their pets will stop at the top of the stairs or at the edge of the couch or bed. They will cock their head and just look for a bit, as if to say that they can't see how far it is. They can't. Going up the stairs or onto the couch is not an issue because the next step or the cushion is right in front of their face and eyes. The distance is easily seen.

With hearing, when we arrive home, we find them asleep when they used to greet us at the door. The earliest stage of hearing loss is occurring when we call them and they don't respond. Invariably, owners feel that their pets are ignoring them or having 'selective hearing'. They aren't, of course, they can't hear you as well as they used to, both in volume and in frequency. Hearing loss for a dog or cat is the same as in a human. Their hearing ability gradually decreases over time. We think it happened all of a sudden because their hearing loss hit a point that it was noticeable to us.

With both vision and hearing, your pet thinks that the world is changing and that they are still normal. The world around them is becoming quieter and foggier. As owners, they think you are getting sneaky. You do startle them when you get home and they didn't hear you until you were in the house. They are thinking, "How did they do that?" Even with acute blindness, animals think someone has simply turned out the lights.

So, how do they deal with it? Dogs and cats will sit down and decide that this is different than it used to be. Then they figure out a new strategy. This is a very healthy attitude. Adopting this attitude is very healthy for us! It is a great response to a change in our pet's lives. They just think it through and figure out a new way to get things done! The world has changed and they are still normal. This is a great response to a change in our lives! If we can't change it, develop a new strategy to get it done!

Humans get new glasses, hearing aids (or not!) and are grumpy about becoming old. We make ourselves miserable by moaning about the changes occurring in our reality. We should be adopting our pet's attitude. Stop moaning, realize that things have changed and develop a new strategy for getting things done. We have a huge advantage over our pets by being able to adjust our environment to help us. If we can change things, we should!

Our pets are teaching us to adjust our attitudes. Purchase your new glasses, your hearing aids, your new hip or knee. Then sit down, think how this is different than it used to be and develop your new strategies for a dynamic future. It's the old, "from this day forward" attitude. Have I said it enough? Then get it done

Aging dogs and cats, as opposed to us, assume they are still normal and the world has changed. This is a critical perception for us to know so we can keep our older pets out of harms way. They will walk into the street in front of a car because they assume they can still hear or see well. They will walk off a deck and crash into the yard. They will miss the last two steps going down the stairs. Remember, they think that the world has changed, they haven't.

When I talk about this topic with clients, I always tell the female human that aging dogs and cats are just like aging men. Aging men assume they are still normal and can do everything they used to do! It's the old "What were you doing up on that roof at your age?" syndrome! Women know truth when they hear it. Men, however, usually don't get it! You need to know about this perception difference in older pets in order to keep them safe. Adapting this 'old dog strategy' is very healthy for us as we age or as 'life happens' to us. Older men think this doesn't apply to them at all!

Dr. J'isms

1. We change as we age.
2. Our pet's world changes as they age.
3. A pet's perception controls their world.
4. Complaining doesn't change our age.
5. New strategies are a healthy aging behavior.
6. Protect your aging pet from its changing world!

FUN PAGE
Your Syndromes

1. Pick 3 topics you have an opinion on.

2. Do research on the 3 topics to find out the facts.

3. Evaluate whether your *perception as reality* opinions fit the facts. Vigorously pursue 'reality' based opinions in your future.

Hannah snoring in one of her sunny spots

Chapter 25

A No Fault Life?

Ouch! That hurt! When an animal bites you, who's fault is it? In some ways this will read like a new topic, but it's actually an extension of perception as our reality that we talked about in the last chapter. The health care team at our hospital was taught that if they are bitten by a dog, cat, pocket pet or snake, it was their fault. The animal was never at fault. When I state this, I usually get inquisitive looks. If an animal bites you, they are just being themselves in an unusual place, for them, under some kind of perceived stress. Remember, perception is reality, to them and to us. When an animal bites you, it's not personal. They are just being themselves in a difficult situation that we understand and they do not.

An animal is never, ever, at fault if you let yourself get bitten. Some people feel that animals should know better. Others thank that they are just mean or nasty. Actually, they are just protecting themselves and hey, who is the higher species here? Which of us has a higher center in our brain that can use logic, understand the situation and act or respond accordingly? It is never the animal's fault. If I am bitten, even if it is an aggressively vicious animal, it is always my fault.

When a patient is hospitalized or boarding in our facility they may become *kennel hostile*. In other words, when in a kennel they act aggressive, may lunge at the door and snap at people on the other side of the kennel door. However, if you open the door, put a leash on them and bring them out, they are fine, normal, tail wagging and no hassle creatures. Why would they react that way.

If you think about it from the animal's perspective or better yet, try it from the animal's point of view. Go to your local veterinarian's office, sit in a kennel and look at the world through their eyes. You'll see someone outside looking in, with a leash and filling up your visual field. You are trapped! You can't run or hide. For all you know, you may be on the verge of being attacked. While this is going through their mind, we open the door and reach for them with a loop! Help! Snap, snap! We think they should know us better but the threat for some animals is real. With time and experience they learn that there is no threat and lose those habits ... usually.

It's the same for all animals, even a cat in a carrier. All they see is a giant hand coming toward them out of the light at the end of the carrier. I might think that biting is a viable option for me under that circumstance. The bottom line is that the animals are just being themselves and reacting to a perceptually stressful situation. Again, it's not personal.

So, if we get bitten, it's our own fault. The damage we receive is directly related to how stupid or inexperienced we have been around that animal. Sorry, but that's just the way it is. Any type of physical retaliation from you only confirms the perception these animals have. You have just confirmed to them that you are scary and out to get them in some way! You are there to cause pain. Remember "chapter 4, Border Collie brains and one trial learners," when it talks about one trial learning. Emotional responses pop open the hard drive of the brain and everything is recorded for future use. These animals never forget a bad situation because it's recorded permanently. If the trauma is bad enough, you will never train them out of the reaction.

Same topic, different species. Think about how this applies to your life when you perceive someone at home or at work has 'bitten' you. Are you looking at the situation with an accurate perception? Do you really need to bite back to protect yourself? When another human being bites you, verbally, emotionally or physically, who's at fault?

The pet analogy should apply and does. Unlike the world of animals, no human can hurt us without our permission. Ok, ok, I know that there are some jerks out there that have whacko behavior, but I'm really referring to our normal, every day life. No one in his or her rationally logical mind would get into a pen with an angry bull! Well, stupid heads or chemically impaired people might consider it but we often find ourselves doing just that in our relationships at home or the workplace.

We can now realize that the person trying to *bite* us verbally, emotionally or physically is just being his or her self under the stress of the moment. Like our pets, it's not you personally that's the issue, it's always the situation. You may just be the one handiest to unload on. The humans we are talking about may be in some kind of kennel or carrier in their own mind. They will react that way at that moment to anyone standing outside their *kennel*. If it's you, whether or not you get bitten and carry scars around, is up to you. Be careful, however, being bitten can become a habit.

Personality Insights, Inc., our D.I.S.C. certification company, teaches that no one is doing anything to us; they are just doing it for themselves or to protect themselves. In other words, they are the dog in the kennel, the cat in the carrier or the bull in the pen. In these events, we are all reacting to the situation, never to the person. Dog, cat, cow, horse or human, the analogy holds up completely. Now, if I keep getting *bitten* over and over and over again, who is being the stupid head?

It helps us to know that it is almost never personal when someone, animal or huma,n bites us. It is nearly always the situation or circumstances. The reactive behavior is out of control, of course, but you don't generally keep pointing a gun at yourself and pulling the trigger after you've been shot once, right? The goal is to learn that we can go through life without faulting others. When we can accept our own actions in a situation, our own life becomes much more enjoyable. There are a lot of different types of abuse, but when it occurs, make sure it doesn't happen to you again and again and again.

Dogs and cats have taught me that you just have to love humans. Do our pets have the same **love** humans have? Who knows, but I do know that their attitudes are always non-judgmental until they have a reason to be wary. I do know that if something causes them pain, they will learn to avoid it quickly and remove it from their life. I repeat. I have learned from your pets that you just have to love humans, but you must protect yourself against some of the jerks and people that are toxic to you.

Animals know that most people are wonderful. Animals know that most people are their friends. Animals know that a few people (and animals) are just jerks and need to be avoided. Avoiding something takes action! Action and avoidance are both "A" words that are easy to remember. The key here is 'avoidance', not confronted, lived with, or volunteer to spend time with. Get out of their way and stay away!!

You can tell that your pets have taught me to love you. You can tell that your pets have taught me that if you're a jerk, I'm going to avoid you. It's a good way to live your life. However, if you can't avoid or escape from a jerk, get some help from somewhere or someone. If you know of animals that can't get away from the jerks in their lives, please, find them some help. We can walk away but the animals can't. We must help.

If you do need to confront a jerk, you will need to stand your ground and if necessary, attack. Jerks can't stand someone that really attacks. I have seen more than one Chihuahua that could back down a Doberman Pinscher just by expressing an attitude. (Remember, avoidance is the action of first choice. It creates a lot less pain.) Don't express an attitude unless you are willing to go to the wall with it. I've seen several one-eyed Chihuahuas that vacillated at the last moment. In life, it's usually best to avoid the jerks unless you like pain. Stay away from them and leave them in the dust.

Dr. Doug Jernigan

Dr. J'isms

1. If you get *bitten* it's your own fault
2. If you keep getting *bitten* you must enjoy it.
3. Love humans; avoid the jerks.
4. Animals have a no-fault life.
5. We can have a no-fault life.
6. The choices are ours.

FUN PAGE
Your No Fault Life

1. Write down 3 situations where you have been *bitten* by someone.
   Ex: Untrue office gossip about you.

2. Analyze each item from list 1 until you can see that it's the situation, not you personally, that has caused the event.

3. List 3 *jerks* that you have left in the dust of your past and consider if there are any others in your life today that need to join them.

A very young Ozzie, the Russian Grizzly Bear, feeling good!

Chapter 26
Feelings, It's All About Feeeeelings!

Feeling bad? Feeling good? Feeling so-so? How do we change the way we feel on command? How we train our dogs to behave works with us.

#1 Change what you are focusing on

Think of a pet from your past or present. Let's use a dog as an example. It is sleeping soundly, snoring away (at least if it's a Dachshund, Beagle or Basset hound), twitching as it lays there, running rabbits in its sleep. You announce, "Come, get dinner!" and bang! You have a dog roaring through the house. Or perhaps, it's our Dachshund, Hannah, wandering through the yard, living through her nose and purposefully ignoring my, "Hannah, come! It's time to go in." She is meandering away or at a parallel to me so I can't get the leash over her head. She won't look directly at me because if she did, she would be disobeying. By not making eye contact she just doesn't know I am trying to get her attention. Hannah's ears didn't always function correctly, either.

Then, I use my aces in the hole, "Hannah, it's time for dinner or Hannah, let's get a treat!" Suddenly, it's a miracle! Her hearing is restored, her brain works and she is no longer disoriented, confused and wandering. In that instant, a long brown rocket dog comes barreling toward me and hits the back door before I do. Yes, if you change what you are focusing on, you change the way you feel, react or respond! You can become a long brown rocket dog in your own life. Just find what represents dinner or treats for you!

#2 Change how you move your body!

A few years ago, someone designed a training leash that now goes by a variety of names. Some of these are the Halty, the Gentle Leader and a myriad of other names. They all work on the same basic principle. They have a collar component with a loop that goes over the top of the nose of a dog (if it has one). This enables the dog to hold its head in a kind of a chin down or level position on its own due to the positioning of the loop and collar. No pain is involved. It is extremely effective behavior control when walking a dog.

Why does this work? When a dog's head is in this position, chin down or level, it creates a much more calm emotional state. When a dog gets excited, the head goes up, the ears go up, it's hair stands on end, the brain lights up, the emotions fire and zoom - we're off and running or barking or pulling on the leash, or wanting to fight.

This training leash keeps the dog from starting that "action cascade" by keeping its head level. The result is a dramatically calmer, controlled dog on a walk. This is effective because in dogs and us, our emotions are directly related to our body posture. The way we move our body creates our emotional state. Our emotional state dictates how we move or hold our body. The relationships between our body, the way we use it and our emotions is hardwired into our brains and available for us to use to our benefit.

If you see someone that is sitting with his head down and their shoulders rounded or drooping, you might conclude that they are sad or feeling down. You would be looking at a bodily reflection of their emotional state. If they were chatting away, laughing, moving their hands around and being very animated, you might assume they are happy and having a good time.

We can assess emotional states by how a person moves or expresses themselves by their body language. In fact, scientific research in humans has shown that how you move muscles of your face has the same direct effect on your emotional state. Think about a dog that is acting aggressive. When the lips curl and the hair stands on end the emotional state is visible. If you smile before you answer the phone, you always sound friendly.

So, here is a good doggone conclusion. If you are feeling emotionally down, change how you move your body into a happy or contented or fired up body movement. You will find that your emotions will, not might or could, but will change. If you want to be sad, make yourself look sad and your emotions will change to sad. It is amazing how this works. It's not a gimmick. You don't have to believe it. It's like gravity. Whether or not you know about it, it affects you. It is physiological. It is reproducible. It can help us when we need it.

The validity of this behavior connection was confirmed to me by your enthusiastic reports about how much your dog improved on your walks when using the aforementioned leash. Most women, after using these leashes on their unruly, willful dogs and watching them become the walking dog of their dreams, wanted to know if I knew if something similar was available for the humans in their lives!

These two techniques will give you complete control over your behavior. Are there other techniques? Sure, but none more effective than these. By applying this little bit of knowledge, your "I didn't feel like doing it" excuse is gone. Using what our pets teach us is a choice. It's our choice because it's our life. If these techniques create a really wonderfully trained dog that is a joy to be around, why not do it to yourself and have a wonderfully joyful and fulfilled life that you choose?!

Dr. J'isms

1. Change your focus, you change your emotions.

2. Body motion and usage control your emotions.

3. You control your body motion and how you use it.

4. You control your emotions.

5. Change how you move, change your emotions.

6. Your emotional state is a choice from now on.

FUN PAGE
Your No Fault Life

1. Stop right now and write down how you feel.

2. Begin to breathe more rapidly, lift up your eyes, smile broadly and lift up your hands in a "*Rocky Balboa*" style. What does it do for your feelings?

3. Most of us have plenty of *downer* feelings. Make a list of 10 motions you can use to blast them away. Think of the last time you were really fired up and what you were doing!

Chapter 27
Die ... t

Dessert!! Finally, we're talking about food! Veterinarians are trained in nutrition. Over the decades, I have followed the research on diets and supplements with a lot of interest. Maybe it's because I am a veterinarian, the son of a veterinarian. Children of veterinarians are raised around animals that need to be fed. In the college of veterinary medicine and in other agricultural disciplines we learn the impact of different diets and different components of diets on blood chemistry, body fat, muscle leanness and health.

What's amazing to me is that with all this knowledge, the number 1 problem in American society for humans or pets is obesity and its medical impact. None of us can brag about how much we know, because even if you know what you should be doing, it doesn't mean you will do it, for you or your pet. It seems that the action step is usually our downfall. So here is this veterinarian's take on diets.

Obesity is always too many calories, period. There is no gray area. Cut to the chase, turn the page and it is always too many calories. The best analogy I learned was the one about receiving a traffic ticket for driving too fast for the existing conditions. Legally, it makes no difference what your speed or the speed limit was. You were ticketed for driving too fast for the existing conditions. Even so, when it comes to our own situation with body fat, we may feel we have unusual circumstances. We may feel it's glandular or hormonal or genetic or whatever. However, if we are gaining weight, it's simply too many calories for the existing conditions. It's simply too many calories for your existing conditions. If we want to lose weight and it isn't happening: it's too many calories for the existing conditions. The end. Full stop. If you think there is a medical basis, get it checked out.

To lose weight, one must consume fewer calories. It is no different whether we have two legs or four. In general, it falls into, "dog food for dogs, cat food for cats, cow food for cows, pig food for pigs, horse food for horses and human food for humans."

This will sound like advertising. Many veterinarians feed the *Hill's Pet Nutrition* diets to their own pets and recommend them for their patients. Why? Simply because they are the best researched and best quality diets on the market. They do not sit on shelves for years letting the nutrients leach out into or puddle onto the bag liners. H.P.N. originated the concept of Prescription diets in the 1940's. When they began to produce *Science Diets* about 30 or so years ago it had a huge impact on the pet food industry. Because H.P.N. diets were so well researched and contain such high quality ingredients, all the pet food companies had to improve their diets to stay competitive.

The result of these improvements is that pets today are living longer, healthier, and higher quality lives across the board. Is this scientifically documented? I don't know, but I saw a lot more very old dogs and very old cats than I saw in the 1970's and 80's. I also realize that part of the phenomenon is that our emotional bond with our pets, the human-animal bond, seems to be greater now than in the past. Because of that emotional bond, we are taking better care of them generally, in addition to the dietary changes. Fewer dogs get H.B.C. (that's hit by cars, trucks would be H.B.T., buses would be H.B.B. and so on) compared to just a few years ago. We are doing a better job all the way around, at least for our pets.

On a daily basis, the single most important healthy thing we can do for our pets is to feed them quality foods. (Oops, do you suppose that applies to us?) So, since you are going to feed them something, feed a diet that is going to keep them healthy and loving you as long as possible! We all love relationships that last.

As I said, we are seeing a lot more very old dogs and very old cats. Physiologically, they look and act younger than their chronological age counterparts did 10-15 years ago. Many of these pets are on H.P.N. and other major brand high quality products and have been for life. I know it's only my anecdotal observation but in more than one presentation I have commented: "If we can do for ourselves what H.P.N. has done for the pets of this world, we would live into our 100's acting like today's 75 year olds."

If diet has that dramatic of an impact for our pets, would we want that for ourselves? Would we like to look, feel and act younger than our chronological age? The key is what we put into our mouths. Yes, I know that smoking is a major player in human health, but this is a chapter on diet. However, the playing field isn't level when it comes to diet for our pets or for us. Humans have a major disadvantage. We have the freedom to control the portions. We control the door to the refrigerator and the keys to the car.

Today we are increasingly making the dash with cash to the fast food stash and teaching our children to do the same! Our youngest generation living today has a projected shorter lifespan than their parents and grandparents. This is appalling. Eating out or carrying in is becoming the rule rather than the exception. However, our dietary rule still applies. If you are gaining weight and body fat, you are driving too many calories for the existing conditions.

There are two attitudes that drive eating habits in both pets and people. All of us either "eat to live" or "live to eat." Many families jokingly fall into the category of humans that live to eat! My family embraced the eat to live category.

For "live to eaters", food is a great time, a reward, social time and something to look forward to. Food comes up in discussions and life events focus around it, "When are we going to eat, what we are going to eat, when do we to shop for food, what's for dessert!?" This attitude doesn't cause you to consume too many calories, it is just an attitude! You choose how much you eat. Food in your stomach is the issue. For 'live to eat' families, eating is family, fellowship, fun and tradition.

When we eat to live, eating and associated food activities are really just a task. Something necessary, something that must be done then dispensed with so you can get onto another project, task, television or party. Eating was just such a task for my Dad and siblings. Our mother even had to create a rule when we hit our teenage years. This was during the late 1950's and early 60's so, of course, we ate at home. Fast food for us was popcorn, ice cream or Chef Boy R De pizza in a box and we had to make the pizza. No, Mom didn't make it, we did! If we wanted to eat fast food, we got to fix it.

The rule was that no one could start to eat until Mother sat down at the table. The reasoning behind the rule was that if we started to eat when she served the food; by the time she could sit down, we (including my Dad) were finished. We were ready to be excused, clear our places, take our dishes to the kitchen and go! Mother didn't like eating alone. She loved having her family around her. It was a good rule and we generally obeyed it. But if Mom wasn't eating with us, the meal was quick! I still don't know if one brother swallowed his peas like pills because he didn't like them or because it was more efficient. For us, Mom sitting down was the starter's gun. The eating was a task to be run.

Family food habits are about traditions and perceptions of reality. My Dad's Dad, the farming grandfather, definitely ate to live. Because of our generational difference, his perceptions were always interesting to me. As he got on in years, he decided to read the Bible, cover to cover. One day when I was helping him at the farm, I asked him what he was learning in his Bible reading. This first thing he said he noticed in the Old Testament was that, "They ate a lot of goat in those days!" I've never heard that preached from a pulpit. Well, maybe it was because he was a farmer that this got his attention. Our perceptions do create our reality.

As an eater, he didn't eat much. He always ate his *All Bran Cereal* for breakfast while complaining about the cost. He knew the exact value of the wheat in the box and could never reconcile the difference between the value of the wheat and the cost of the cereal. In his opinion, farmers always got the short end of the income stick. Farmers today would still agree with him. The contents of a moderate meal delivered by the Senior Citizens group would provide him the rest of his day's calories. My Granddad Jernigan had opinions about food. He was very picky about what and how much he ate. Today, he is a good example of what dietary caloric restriction research is finding. This research shows that the less you eat, the longer you live. Genetics are important and so is exercise, of course.

When we finally had to put him into a retirement home, he only complained about two things.

1. They were trying to kill him with the huge volume of food they wanted him to eat. The volume, in his opinion, was way too much. Uh, hello, America!

2. They wanted him to eat food that was green (you, know lettuce, green peppers, green beans, peas etc.) and he wouldn't eat anything green! Well, at least one of his complaints made sense. This man was still feeding his cattle (using tractors and hydraulics) when he was nearly 94. He became one of the role models in my life for the eat to live philosophy. He lived to within a month of 99. My oldest grandson was born 6 months before my grandfather died. If my grandson lives as long as his great-great grandfather did, it'll represent nearly 200 years of Jernigan history.

When you look at North American's behavior, we appear to be mostly live to eaters. All you have to do is open your ears to what people are discussing around you at work, at play, at home, on television, on the radio, at school and everywhere, it's seemingly all about food.

We love food but we don't like what is happening to us. We are trying to reduce. We want the next, newest diet. We want detail and structure. We want the lowest calorie diet. We want, and actually most of us need, for medical reasons, a pill or surgery or, or, or, or whatever is the next new thing to get rid of all those unwanted, unhealthy extra pounds that were so much fun to put on and are so hard to take off.

Yet, in spite of all this, we still consume too many calories for our existing conditions. While it may sound simplistic, the next few sentences are all you need to join your pets in high energy, health and long life! If humans would just eat real food, with a few antioxidants, primarily a daily vitamin, Vitamin C, Vitamin E and some source of calcium, our entire physiology would change to a healthy state, quickly. Does it take some time? Sure! Can you do it? Sure! Is it simple? Sure! Is it easy? No! It will take some goal setting, daily habits changed, planning ahead in the beginning and some persistence. Here is the human diet a veterinarian would recommend!

Eat real food. We need some source of protein with veggies, fruits, nuts and berries as close to their natural state as we can safely consume them. Is it that simple? Yes. Is it more expensive than the 'dash with cash to the fast food stash? No! Add up your time, your fuel cost, the actual food cost, the waiting in line cost, the cold you got from the person behind you in line cost, the medical bills for diagnostic tests for chronic degenerative diseases cost and the prescription drug cost.

When computed on a monthly basis, I think you can afford to eat real food. Watch "Super size me!" You probably have the cash flow for real food, real energy, real health and a much longer, higher quality life. Here is the bottom line. Do what is listed above and you will change your life span and health.

Even as I am writing this, I just came from a local pizzeria (Didn't I say you could have a rare treat?) and noticed 3 things:
1. Teenagers working behind the counter all appeared lean.
2. The people eating in front of the counter were all very broad across the beam (mostly, way too heavy).
3. I've learned to love people, but they reminded me of the hogs I watched as a kid on the farms. The people in front of the counter looked like they were at a hog trough. The image keeps me from buffet style restaurants. I'm sure they are very nice hogs, very sincere hogs, good family hogs but behaviorally; they are beginning to look like what they eat! I've always liked the phrase, "Nothing tastes as good as lean feels!"

For me, it's time to start, "looking at myself when I eat", see what I eat, see how much I eat and see which trough I'm eating out of! How about you? You can't just exercise yourself to leanness. Recent studies show that exercise is an important factor to help your body function, but calories in, calories worn, is the cut-to-the-chase, bottom line reality. Exercise for health! Eat for leanness!

I've always believed that the human long distance runners were the 'eat to live' body style. I realized, after running a lot in my early years, that the really lean, average citizen, long distance runner was either too tired or felt too bad to eat very much. Ok, I'm joking but either way, they didn't eat much! Some, on the other hand, ran long, hard and fast daily so they could eat a lot of calories. If they ever stopped running though, hello, fat! Calories in are far more important than massive quantities of exercise. Do you need to exercise? Yes, lightly, moderately or vigorously, do something aerobically, use some weights and do it regularly.

It dawned on me while writing this, that Mama Cass' body style in the 1960's (of *Mamas and Papas* fame) was the rarity. Today, her body style is all around us! It might even be in our mirrors. Open your eyes and look! If you aren't losing weight and you want to, you need fewer calories. If you are gaining weight and don't want to, you need fewer calories. It doesn't have to be a lot fewer, but it does have to be fewer. Remember, to get lean, you must consume fewer calories than your existing conditions call for!

Here is the last note on this topic. Clients with overweight pets always receive this advice. I tell them to feed their pets on a schedule, measure their pet's existing food volume, reduce that volume by 10-25%, but do not change the routine. Dogs and cats are creatures of habit. They really don't care how much they get of something, only that they get it on time. If the condition warrants it, I'll recommend "light" diets so they get the same volume of food, but with fewer calories.

We are similar. Eat your normal schedule. Begin to modify what and how much you eat. Please, make it a task, not a pleasure. Finally, start to get some exercise. If you will do what you have just read – Action, then the lean *feeling good* future is yours.

Dr. J'isms

1. Do you *live to eat* or *eat to live*?

2. Calories in are calories worn.

3. Stop the *dash with cash to the fast food stash*!

4. Start the *dash with cash to the real food stash*!

5. Too many calories for the existing conditions creates obesity.

6. Fewer calories than needed for existing conditions create leanness.

7. Exercise is good for health, not weight loss.

8. If you can control your pet's food, control yours!

Ok, we've killed the diet issue, but the health issue is linked, so here is some "food" for thought! People have a tendency to say, "Dr. so and so cured my pet or my pneumonia, etc." Unfortunately, this attitude hinders relationships with health care professionals and creates stereotypes that just aren't true. We shouldn't put our "Dr." types (including veterinarians) up on a pedestal but they should be a vital, sometimes critical, part of our health care team. Their skills are needed, but it's our health. When we go to their offices, we are inviting them to join our team. They are the specifically trained professionals, but we should be in charge. All decisions are yours. It would help most of us to have a better perspective and be more assertive about our own health care if we realized what the reality about healing really is. We aren't changing what occurs in your medical care, just your perception of what is occurring. This perceptual reframe or change in perception will put you in the driver's seat of your own and your pet's health care. Is this just my opinion? Of course it is. Will it help you? Yes. See if this makes sense.

As a young veterinarian, I had a client thank me for curing their pet. As I puffed up in my own mind about a successful outcome, I realized the fallacy of my response and the inaccuracy of their perception. It was a defining moment for me. My knowledge had helped, of course, but their pet had healed on its own. The truth about what occurs with healing really freed me from my medical ego and any self-importance I may have felt. At that moment, I became a team member with you and your pet.

Medical people, whether with humans or pets, create an environment, using surgery, chemicals and drugs, within which the body can heal. If the body's primary ability to heal itself in some manner is gone then there is not a lot anyone can do. Sometimes, the environment we create is quite dramatic and critical to survival but if the body can't do its own thing eventually…death happens. By the same token, medical people can't 'save' you, no matter what you hear on television commercials. We can only extend life, hopefully, with a quality worth living.

Cancer is a great analogy. If the body's immune system is working properly, it identifies the abnormal cells, destroys them and you don't get cancer. This occurs 24/7. When cancerous cells aren't identified and then grow out of control, you have cancer. Cancer therapy is designed to do what the body didn't or couldn't. This therapy is designed to destroy the cancer cells in the hope that the body will keep it in check in the future.

Unfortunately, the cancer allowing defect is in the immune system and we are still working on creating the environment to repair a defective immune system. They are getting close in a few areas. Cancer research is very exciting with new frontiers being reached nearly every day. When we figure out how to restore the immune system, we'll have a cancer "cure." As a prostate cancer survivor, I can only urge you to do the tests your physicians recommend and catch anything sneaking up on you early.

Speaking about cancer, there are some neat things that they are finding out through research with ill dogs. For example: Most malignant cancers are sugar-sucking machines. They take energy away from the body and then generate excess lactic acid (this is like cancer poop), which is then dumped into the system and the body has to metabolize it. So the body has its regular energy usage, is losing energy to the cancer and has an increased workload getting rid of the extra lactic acid. This one, two, three punch is an extra load as to what is normal. A normal person only has his/her regular energy usage. The cancer patient has an additional two ways that energy is burned up. This is why people with systemic cancers lose weight quickly. It's why you hear, "Did you see so and so? He or she is so thin. The cancer must be eating them alive." It is.

Research in pets show that if you can eliminate sugar from the diet and go to a protein, fat and insoluble fiber diet, some of these systemic cancers are hindered or even regress. In nearly all cases, the life span is increased over pets whose diets don't change. Please note, they still died of cancer. Dogs and humans are different, but it is exciting watching the research results that are coming to a medical office near you. Early detection gives you the best outcomes.

There is a lot of discussion right now in life about health options. One well-proven factor is that we all eat way too much sugar. So, as surgeons used to say, before M.R.I., C.T. and P.E.T. scans), "When in doubt, cut it out!" Please, don't feed the cancer! This applies to sugar in all human and animal diets. Sugar is a carbohydrate. A carbohydrate's only purpose in our diets is for energy. A recent veterinary lecturer made an accurate statement that is easy to remember, "With carbohydrates, you either burn them or you wear them!" Eliminating or reducing sugar and processed carbohydrates is as important to you as stopping smoking.

Finally, one of the medical axioms we healthcare professionals subscribe to is, "First, do no harm!" We have all been taught that the body is an amazing vehicle. It has systems, sub-systems, micro-systems, macro-systems, integrated systems, synergistic systems, antagonistic systems and feedback loops, just to name a few. Even under the worst circumstances, your body can perform well, as long as everything is working at some level. Abuse it and you lose it!

The point of all of this is to remember –when you or your pet is getting medical care, the goal is to create an environment that will allow the body to repair itself. Your health care team, for you or your pet, should be just that, a team, with you as the most important part. My brother, a physician and my registered nurse relatives would be the first to urge you to be an advocate for your health. No one else lives in your body! I know that you must be an advocate for your pet. No one else cares about your pet the way you do. And as always, prevention is the best treatment.

Dr. J'isms

1. Everything heals in the right environment.
2. Malignant cancers are sugar-sucking machines.
3. You are responsible for your health.
4. Less sugar, better health!

FUN PAGE
Your Die ... t

1. Make a list of 10 attitudes you have about food.

2. Label each attitude with either 'eat to live' or 'live to eat.'

3. For 3 days, write down what you eat and label each item as *real food* or *fast food*. Then change your shopping lists to real food. Simple, huh! Lean is coming!

How many dogs are here and in the world? Too many.

Two cute kittens can produce how many? Too many.

Chapter 28
Sex And The Single Dog

"Where is the sex? You've got to have sex!" A friend of mine said this while looking at my list of topics. Well, he was right. Of course, it was a guy. I hadn't gotten there because the topic doesn't really have anything to do with a Border collie brain (wrong!). However, I simply cannot create a book about humans and animals without addressing sex.

There are too many pets in the world that get euthanized, so, please, don't breed any more. Daily, across the US, tens of thousands of dogs and cats are put down, killed (hopefully, humanely) because they don't have any homes or someone to love them. Most of them have lived with some kind of suffering or neglect before they wind up in a shelter. Like it or not, that is the fact. There are people working in animal shelters, loving people, who look into these animal's eyes for the last time and then, poof, they're gone. Some shelters are "no-kill" but it means that other shelters have to do their killing for them.

The problem is that you aren't getting the job done. You just don't get it. You stop breeding pets and the problem goes away. Animal over-population isn't an animal problem. It's a people problem. If every qualified veterinarian in North America did nothing but surgical sterilizations 24/7, we would still lose the pet population battle under the existing conditions. How do we know this? The Humane Society of the U.S. web site (www.hsus.org) lists the grim facts, "In just 6 short years, one female dog and her puppies will create 67,000 new dogs. In just 7 short years, one female cat and her kittens will create 420,000 new cats." Obviously, veterinarians, rescue organizations, humane societies and the pets, need your help.

There is no expense in keeping your animal away from the opposite sex during the (usually) two 3 week seasonal cycles (dogs) a year. Cats, on the other hand, keep cycling in heat (about 7 days in, 7 days out) until they are bred. They ovulate spontaneously when bred, so they need the male to end the cycle with a pregnancy. They can also spontaneously end their cycle, but it's uncommon. However, keeping your cat indoors without access to males create no kittens!

The other alternative is to have them surgically neutered. Duh! Your local veterinarian can get you the facts and fees. I know we all hate the thought of putting our pets through a surgical procedure but it needs to be done. With peri-operative pain medications, most of our patients are up and about within 24-48hrs. If only we could do so well. Much research is being done to make chemical sterilization safer, cheaper and easier, but it's not perfected yet. There are still too many risks in animals. If each of us does what we can in our communities, we can stop the suffering for these sweet creatures but it takes all of us.

So, now you have a dog and you will not neuter it. Fair enough! Men have the biggest issue with the thought of neutering their male pet. Older male dogs get prostate disease, but rarely prostate cancer. Benign prostatic hyperplasia with increasing age is the biggest issue in intact male dogs. They respond to the seasonal pheromones that float for miles from the females that are in heat ... and bingo, they develop a large one - prostate, that is. That prostate creates problems because of the increase in size and pressure on the urethra. They have difficulty urinating, may get constipated or develop perianal hernias. This is in addition to the *desire* factor of wanting to breed and the behaviors that go with it.

The solution to all these medical issues is to have them neutered. If you eliminate the hormone testosterone by 98%, the adrenal gland still produces trace amounts, everything shrinks. It's similar to when *Viagra* leaves the system, only neutering is permanent. In dogs, for the discriminating client, *Neuticles*, a synthetic testicular prosthesis can be implanted and if installed properly, they won't generally "click" when the dog walks or runs! You can give your dog "the look," but none of the hassle! And, yes, I suppose you could have bigger ones installed than the originals so all the other males would have Neuticle envy!

I know that last bit sounds strange, but while sex and humans is complicated. Sex and the single dog is pretty straight forward. Women, without a question, have their female dogs spayed and their male dogs castrated when recommended by their veterinarian. As I said, men are a whole 'nother world when it comes to neutering their male pets. Oh, sure, spay the female but leave my male, dog that is, alone. I recommend that women tell their human males at home that we are recommending neutering their pet, not them!

Veterinarians can't work on humans, of course, but some of you males out there need to work on your manners and relationships with women. From the attitudes I have seen expressed in my exam room, many of the women in your lives would schedule you tomorrow for the surgery we have been discussing if they could do it legally without your permission!

Back to dogs! When the females are in heat, the intact males react to the scent in the air! They pace, they drool, they walk by the windows, they walk by the door with a deep inhale underneath it. They sigh and quit eating or eat less. They have such a sad look in their eyes. In fact, you can see the same look in the eyes of any single human male sitting in a bar on a Friday night!

Owners will bring their dogs in because they are acting strange or NDR, you know, "not doing right"! I usually listen to the history, do a good clinical exam and knowing that females are in heat around the city, I can easily diagnose the cause of their *dis-ease*. The treatment is either to neuter them or to have the clients be patient.

It's important that you don't let these males get loose outdoors. Traditionally, the *in heat* of year is when the H.B.C. traumas increase. When sex is on the mind, dogs and cats think this way, "Car? What car? Crunch!" Please protect your pets and don't ever let them run loose. It's a dangerous world for our roaming pets any time of the year.

The *heat season* in an area usually occurs for about a 6 to 8 week time frame in the spring and fall. Also, during this time, males may become more aggressive, irritable, pick fights, and act obnoxious by anointing in all the wrong places. In other words, like men in any bar on any given night anywhere in North America when single women walk in! I tell clients that if they want to understand their intact male pet's behavior they should go to any bar and watch the men. It's always entertaining and usually instructive. As I said earlier, they will see the same behavior in the men they see in their intact male dog during breeding season. Really, try it some time. Just go sit in a bar, without participating, of course, and watch humans behave!

Finally

The last word on sex and the single dog. The oldest fallacy is that if a female dog has a litter, it makes her into a better pet. Well, whoop-de-do! If it works for dogs, it must work for humans. Every woman that has children must be a better wife and human being than those that don't, right? Well, the analogy is solid but you can see that it's an old wives tale.

What has happened to your logic? Where is the higher center of your brain? The reason this myth has evolved over the years is because the average dog comes into heat at about 7-9 months of age, depending on the size and breed. The giant breeds and the tiny or teacup breeds usually are older for their first heat cycle. Seldom are they bred then or during the next cycle. Then when the dog is about 15-18 months old, they are bred. Whatever rationale is given for breeding, it is outdated.

Mom, usually, wants the kiddos to watch the 'miracle of birth' or some such antiquated idea. Really, if you want your children to see the miracle of birth, them sneak them into a human delivery room and watch your own species being born. That ought to cure 'em and help decrease the human population boom! However, the pet gets pregnant and about 60 days later, 63 days for dogs, for you detailed, High C style people, and bingo, we have puppies or kittens or whatever. Isn't it great?

The puppies or kittens begin to be weaned within 5-6 weeks and go to new homes, right? I will add that if you breed them, you bought them. Please, find them good homes, preferably before you breed them, so they don't wind up with a short life at a shelter. At this time your, now, Momma dog, is about 2 years old and her personality is wonderful. Surprise!

If you had her spayed at an early age, then when she becomes two or three years old, her personality changes and "voila!" they are wonderful. Age is the factor, not having puppies! So, please, don't breed our pets for the kiddies. There are wonderful television programs and D.V.D.'s to further their education on this topic. I might also add, that if your pet's personality doesn't settle down by the age of 2 or 3, then it will by the time they are 13 or 14 years old. That's not a typo, it's just a fact, Jack! Enjoy your pets, but don't breed them, there are just too many animals in the world that need loving homes. Could

Dr. J'isms

1. Humans cause surplus pets.

2. Humans cause the euthanasia of surplus pets.

3. Humans cause problems.

4. Human birth, not animal birth, should be watched by children!

5. Age creates great personality, not litters.

6. No breeding? No problems!

FUN PAGE
Sex And...

1. Get on the Internet and search humane societies or dog and cat rescues for the facts of pet overpopulation. Block out 30 minutes and go for it.

2. Over the next 3 days, work this info into your conversations to raise awareness of the problems. Everyone loves to talk about dogs and cats.

3. 1 and 2 are a little action oriented. If we don't care, no one will.

Mama Wise with her family of Jack Russell Terriers. A photo is the only way to make J.R.T.'s stop moving.

Chapter 29

Terrier Bliss

Let's talk about terriers and mice! Let's talk about us, too! Let's go back to how our brains are like Border Collies and maybe we can become the "successful Terrier" we want to be.

Any breed that has Terrier in its name – Rat, Toy, Jack Russell, Cairn, Scottish, West Highland, and so forth, came from de-mousing stock. They are the original de-ratters. They live to kill rodents. If you ever see a Terrier working a room, they move like lightning and cover a lot of square footage in a hurry. You may think it's your kitchen or your family room but to a Terrier it's just potential mouse turf. Terriers know there must be mice somewhere. From their birth until they die they are on a hunt. They know mice are quick, but they are quicker. They know mice are cunning, but they are quicker. They know mice can bite, but they are quicker.

See the theme? Quickness means that you get mice! Why? So they can eat them!! Gross!! For dogs, it's not a game. For dogs, it's a lifestyle. This is the 'dash with cash to the fast food stash!' We're talking a real treat. Find it, catch it, kill it, eat it and leave the tail hanging out of your mouth! Wow! If you saw this happen, most of us would think it was quite gross. It all ends when that tail is the last thing to go slithering down. Ugh. But look in that Terrier's eyes and you will see only fulfilled bliss. It's a real terrier Zen moment. What a moment to be a Terrier! What a day to be a Terrier! Life is Terrier perfect!

Hopefully, mouse nose, tail and toes are not your passion and not what drives you every day! Here is the point. Every day of their lives, terriers are de-mousing. Their first thought in the morning, the last at night and in their dreams, it's all mouse, rat, mole and vole!

There is a lesson here for us! We could be Terriers! At least, we could act like Terriers! We can find what really gets us inspired. To makes us want to act like Terriers on the hunt, we must find out what gets us, "all fired up!" Wow, what a world it would be, for us personally and all those lives we touch. You may not look like a Terrier or even feel like a Terrier but you can act like one. Find your own mice, rats, moles and voles! They exist in your life. You already have those instincts. You just need to develop your quickness. Find your passion. Find your own mice, rats, moles and voles! Act on it! Act on it! Act on it! Keep acting on it until you can look in the mirror and see, "Terrier fulfilled bliss" in your own eyes every day of the week. Listen to what is inside of you that rings your bell and attracts your attention! What is it that creates your personal passion? When you find the mice, rats, moles and voles in your life, you have found the rest of your life!

Dr. Doug Jernigan

Dr. J'isms

1. Terriers have a passion.
2. Terriers are quick.
3. Humans have passions.
4. Humans can be quick.
5. Action brings you your mice, rats, moles and voles!

FUN PAGE
Your Lifetime Bliss!

1. List 3 things you really, really, really love to do. Ex. Go to the movies.

2. Under each item of list 1. write down any job or career associated with that item. Ex. Projectionist, ticket taker, producer, film editor, script writer, actor, distribution manager, carpet sweeper, etc.

3. Consider a job/career change. Chase your mouse and have fun in your life!

Is this a *new day* or the *same day*?

Summary
Life Happens?

Like a dog in a pasture, the theme running through this book is that the present and your future are up to you. It's the old, "From this day forward!" Sure, life happens, but where you go and what you do is really up to you. You get to make the changes. Most of the changes we want to make start like the proverbial snowball that is rolled from the top of a mountain. As it goes down, it gets larger, faster and clears everything out of its way until it becomes an avalanche! When it finally gets to its goal, the bottom of the mountain, the onetime snowball has real impact! Our lives are the same. Do we want to create a significant impact or just create chaotic impacts within our lives and all those around us?

When you train a puppy, you may need to start over and start over and then start over. In our life and with our Border Collie brains, we may need to start over, start over, and then, finally, start over once again. We may have to go back to the basics at times. We may get frustrated, angry or depressed. We may have to change directions or techniques. If we have patience and fun with a new puppy in it's training, we need to have patience and fun in our own training. Sure, life happens, but are we going to be like a pinball and ricochet off our *life happens* stuff and get ever closer to our goals, or just roll down the game of life and then disappear? If it's good for your dog or cat, it is equally good for you! If you can train your dog or a cat or a horse or a goat or a child, you can train your own brain to get what you want in life: legally, morally and without fat or sugar! Give it a go! These chapters are really daily essays, some short and some longer, to teach you about your relationships with your pet, yourself and the world around you! This "cut to the chase" knowledge combined with action can change your life. ACTING ON NEW KNOWLEDGE creates impact and eventual success. Our pets have taught us a lot. Have a great future. Have the future you choose!!

Dr. J'isms

1. The past is past!

2. Today and the future are yours.

3. Life happens! So?

4. Start over as needed.

5. Have patience and fun with your brain.

6. Train your brain.

7. Have the future you want!

8. Don't be just a Border Collie!

Dr. Doug Jernigan lives in Innisfil, Ontario, Canada with his wife and their four-legged children Dickon, Tucker and Pippin. To connect with Dr. J., go to www.BorderCollieBrain.com

Made in the USA
Lexington, KY
09 October 2017